Elia Chair Publication Series No. 1

Italian-Canadian Studies: A Select Bibliography

Compiled by

Franc Sturino

Mariano A. Elia Chair in
Italian-Canadian Studies
York University
and

The Multicultural History Society of
Ontario

Canadian Cataloguing in Publication Data

Sturino, Franc, 1948-
    Italian-Canadian studies

(Elia Chair publication series ; no. 1)
ISBN 0-919045-37-5

1. Italian Canadians - Bibliography.* 2. Italians - Canada -
Bibliography. I. Multicultural History Society of Ontario. II.
York University (Toronto, Ont.). Mariano A. Elia Chair in
Italian-Canadian Studies. III. Title. IV. Series.

Z1395.I8S78 1988   016.3058'51'0971   C88-093581-2

ISBN: 0-919045-37-5
©1988 Franc Sturino

Contents

Acknowledgement

The production of a bibliography, like other academic publications, requires much discussion and consultation to be transformed from an idea into a reality. Along the way, in preparing the present volume many individuals have contributed of their time and expertise. In particular, the support of the Multicultural History Society of Ontario has been instrumental in helping to bring the project to fruition. I am especially indebted to the Society's academic director, Robert Harney, and to Jean Burnet, Anne McCarthy and Ewald Schaefer for their advice and patience.

Among my colleagues at York University, special thanks goes to Roberto Perin, Clifford Jansen and Tom Traves. Lily Cappodocia, as assistant to the Elia Chair in Italian-Canadian Studies, was conscientious as well as cheerful in working with me on all facets of this compilation, no mean task to be sure. Thanks is also extended to Nicoletta Serio of the University of Milan and to Ivan Basar of the National Library of Canada for their bibliographic assistance.

What strengths and utility the reader finds in this catalogue will be due to the cooperative spirit of the many people whose support made this volume possible.

Introduction

The publication of this bibliography occurs at an important juncture in the development of Italian-Canadian studies and Canadian ethnic studies generally. In any scholarly field such a venture is a sort of rite of passage offering concrete evidence that it has reached a sufficient level of maturity to be taken seriously. This is now certainly the case with the study of Canadian ethnocultural groups, and it is specifically so with the study of Italian Canadians, whose presence in Canada stretches back to the French regime and who now constitute Canada's fourth largest group, 750,000 as of 1981.

Although there has been a tendency in established academic circles to view ethnocultural studies as potentially parochial, filiopietistic or simply irrelevant, implicit in the publication of this bibliography is the belief that ethnocultural studies, done in a scholarly and impartial manner, has its place in history, the social sciences and various humanist disciplines. Just as women's studies or labour studies, for instance, have recently spotlighted the experience of women and workers in Canada's past and present, ethnocultural research puts the focus on a large field of daily experience which was often left out of academic writing. Inasmuch as these and related fields of study have as their common object a better knowledge of society and of people, such investigations interact and enrich one another. Ethnocultural studies, far from threatening to fragment knowledge, promise to deepen our knowledge of Canada.

Of late, a number of scholars, such as historian Robert F. Harney and sociologist Clifford J. Jansen have suggested that Italian Canadians, both by virtue of their numbers and integration into the fabric of Canadian life are no longer an "ethnic group," inasmuch as that term may denote a struggling minority status. It can be said that as a significant and more or less accepted element in the cultural mix of Canada, like Canadians of French, British and Ukrainian origins, Italian Canadians are now part of the nation's landscape. If this is so, they are certainly the most recent to attain such a status. For that reason, the literature about their experience may be instructive for more recently settled or smaller groups in Canada, especially those whose migration patterns and cultural origins are analogous. The present bibliography then should be seen not as the preserve of a particular ethnocultural group, but as a guide to a chapter of a larger story which is part and parcel of Canadian history.

In 1969 the Royal Commission on Bilingualism and Biculturalism lamented the dearth of research about Canadian ethnocultural groups. Since then the field has made great advances. In two decades much has been accomplished and ethnic studies have been conducted in many disciplines: history, sociology, anthropology, psychology, education and literature. The first part of this bibliography has been organized with these disciplinary divisions in mind, although the three sections comprising this part follow from the thematic content of the individual references rather than from an ordering by discipline.

The most sustained effort at documenting the Italian presence in Canada has been carried out by historians. In this work, especially in the writing of Canadian social history, the themes of immigration and ethnicity have held a conspicuous place. As a consequence, historical studies (Section 1) constitute the largest category of references in this bibliography. Moreover, I have devoted a separate section (6) to contemporaneous reports on Italians in Canada published between 1902 and 1927 in the regular bulletin of the Emigration Commissariat of the Italian Ministry of Foreign Affairs (*Bollettino dell'Emigrazione*). These accounts present a view from the opposite side of the Atlantic of the Italian past in Canada which complements Canadian materials.

Sections 2 and 3 of the bibliography deal with the more contemporary experience. Section 2 treats topics such as cultural persistence and change, socio-economic status, family and kinship, literature and folklore. Essentially, it deals with the social and cultural life of Italian Canadians in the post-World War Two period. Section 3 has a more specific focus, consisting of studies related to the question of immigrant and second-generation adjustment. In the main, this section brings together literature on education and socialization.

Although most of the entries in the first three sections refer to works by academics, much serious study has also been done on the Italian-Canadian experience by those outside universities. Such work is also noted. Although the majority of references are to studies which deal specifically with Italian Canadians, others are to more general studies of ethnicity which, however, incorporate Italian Canadians as part of their discussion. The tendency was to include borderline studies that might prove useful. The bibliography lists only published works, with two exceptions. Papers delivered under government auspices or sponsored by the Elia Chair in Italian-Canadian Studies are included since their public access could be guaranteed. To complement the entries referring to published works in the first four sections, Section 5 lists doctoral and masters theses dealing with Italian Canadians.

Section 4 represents a selection of popular non-fiction accounts about Italian Canadians. It lists as many of the more substantial and accessible items as possible, including articles which have appeared in Canadian periodicals. Since the main purpose of the bibliography is to bring together the current store of knowledge on Italian Canadians as constructed or gathered by scholars and researchers, primary source material such as newspapers, Italian-language periodicals and archival collections are not included. Readers interested in popular press reports are referred to the *Canadian Newspaper Index* and *Canadian Periodical Index* published on a regular basis. General references to Italian language and Italian-Canadian periodicals can be found in Section 7.

Although literary criticism and language studies are included, the bibliography omits references to fiction and poetry on the Italian Canadian experience. The omission of fiction and poetry should not be taken as a judgment on their value as a source in scholarly analysis, but rather reflects the fact that some good guides to Italian-Canadian writing have already appeared in print, and these are listed in Section 7. The interested reader will find in this last section references to other bibliographies and guides to various aspects of the Italian New World experience.

This bibliography, then, represents a systematic search of the literature on Italian Canadians up to summer 1987. As a selected bibliography, it makes no claim to being exhaustive. If it offers interested researchers and a more general audience a starting point to rewarding explorations about Italians in Canada and about the variety of Canadian life, it will have served its purpose.

Franc Sturino
Department of History, Atkinson College
Mariano A. Elia Chair in Italian-Canadian Studies
York University

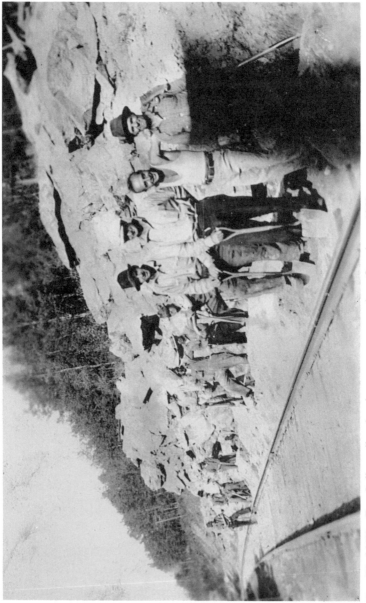

Post-World War Two Italian railroad maintenance crew, northern Ontario, c. 1952

SECTION 1:
HISTORICAL AND RELATED STUDIES

Allen, Glyn P. "Italians in Canada." Paper presented on behalf of the Citizenship Branch, Department of the Secretary of State to the American Italian Historical Association Meeting, Toronto, December 1967. 11 leaves. Typescript.

Amat di San Filippo, Ietro. *Biografia dei viaggiatori italiani e bibliografia delle loro opere.* Rome, 1875.

Antonietti, Sandro. "Emigrazione agricola dall' Italia in Canada". *Rivista di economia agraria* 8 (March 1953): 133-49.

Appunti di lezioni sulla pratica assistenza dell'emigrante tenute nel Pontificio Collegio per l'emigrazione a sacerdoti in cura d'anime. Parte 3: "Preparazione religiosa dell'emigrante-Stati Uniti e Canada." Alessandria: La Popolare, 1924. 192pp.

Armstrong, Fred. "The Second Great Fire of Toronto 19-20 April 1904." *Ontario History* 40 (March 1978): 3-38.

Arnopoulos, Sheila. "Immigrants and Women: Sweatshops of the 1970s." In *The Canadian Worker in the Twentieth Century,* pp. 203-15. Edited by Irving Abella and David Miller. Toronto: Oxford University Press, 1978. Reprint of articles from *Montreal Star* (1974).

Artistic Woodwork Strike 1973. Pamphlet no. 1. Toronto: Right To Strike Committee, [1973]. 28pp.

Avery, Donald. "Canadian Immigration Policy and the 'Foreign' Navvy 1896-1914." *Canadian Historical Association Historical Papers* (1972): 135-56.

Avery, Donald. *"Dangerous Foreigners": European Immigrant Workers and Labour Radicalism in Canada 1896-1932.* Toronto: McClelland and Stewart, 1979. Chaps. 1 and 2.

Baldacci, Osvaldo. "Osservazioni sull'emigrazione calabrese." *Almanacco Calabrese* anno 22-23, no. 22-23 (1973): 131-37.

Barabino, B. "La prima spedizione italiana alla Terra di Baffin." *Rivista Mensile del Club Alpino Italiano* 94, no. 5 (1973): 232-42.

Beazley, Charles Raymond. *John and Sabastian Cabot. The Discovery of North America.* London, 1898.

Bell, Margaret. "Toronto's Melting-Pot." *Canadian Magazine* 41, no. 3 (July 1913): 234-43.

Benoit, Monique, and Scardellato, Gabriele. "L'Archivio Segreto Vaticano: una fonte fondamentale per la storia canadese." *Annali Accademici Canadesi* 1 (Autumn 1985): 49-67.

Bosa, Peter. "Perché e importante conoscere la nostra storia: Giovanni Caboto." *Il Veltro* 1-2, anno XXIX (January-April 1985): 47-51.

Bothwell, Robert, and English, John. "Dirty Work at the Crossroads: New Perspectives in the Riddell Incident." *Canadian Historical Association Historical Papers* (1972): 263-85.

Bradwin, Edmund. *The Bunkhouse Man: A Study of Work and Pay in the Camps of Canada, 1903-1914.* New York: ColumbiaUniversity Press, 1928; reprint ed., Toronto: University of Toronto Press, 1972. 249pp.

Brandenburg, Broughton. *Imported Americans: the Story of the Experiences of a Disguised American and his Wife Studying the Immigration Question.* New York: Fred A. Stokes, 1904, pp. 39-41, 50-52, 101-03. Includes documents from immigration officials.

Brantford and District Citizenship Council. *History of Ours: French, German, Hungarian, Italian, Polish, Ukrainian.* Brantford, Ontario, 1967. 66pp.

Bressani, Francesco. *Relazione delle missioni dei Gesuiti nella nuova Francia.* Macerata, 1653.

Briani, Vittorio. "The Italians Abroad." *Research Digest* 6, no. 4 (1960): 24.

Briani, Vittorio. *Il Lavoro Italiano Oltremare.* Rome: Ministero Affari Esteri, 1975. Chap. 10 on Canada.

Bridle, Augustus. "The Drama of the 'Ward'." *Canadian Magazine* 34, no. 1 (November 1909): 3-8.

Bruti Liberati, Luigi. *Il Canada, l'italia e il fascismo, 1919-1945.* Rome: Bonacci Editore, 1984. 256pp.

Bruti Liberati, Luigi. "Fascismo, antifascismo e gli italiani in Canada." *Italian Canadiana* 2, no. 1 (Spring 1986): 50-62.

Bruti Liberati, Luigi. "Le relazioni tra Canada e Italia e l'emigrazione italiana nel primo Novecento." *Studi Emigrazione/Etudes Migrations* no. 77 (March 1985): 44-67.

Bruti Liberati, Luigi. "Le relazioni tra Italia e Canada nel novecento (1900-1945)." *Il Veltro* 1-2, anno XXIX (January-April 1985): 91-106.

Bureau of Municipal Research. *What Is "The Ward" Going To Do With Toronto?* Toronto: Bureau of Municipal Research, 1918. 75pp.

Burnet, Jean. "Multiculturalism, Immigration, and Racism: A Comment on the Canadian Immigration and Population Study." *Canadian Ethnic Studies* 7, no. 1 (1975): 35-39.

Cabrini, Angelo. *Emigrazione ed emigranti.* Bologna: Zanichelli, 1911. Pt. 2.

Canada. Department of Citizenship and Immigration. "Across Canada." *Canadian Welfare* 35 (March 1959): 86-87.

Canada. Citizenship Branch. Department of Citizenship and Immigration. *Notes on the Canadian Family Tree.* Ottawa: Queen's Printer, 1960. 137pp.

Canada. Department of External Affairs. "Relations between Canada and Italy." *External Affairs* 17, no. 12 (December 1965): 524-30.

Canada. Department of Labour. *The Royal Commission Appointed to Inquire into the Immigration of Italian Labourers to Montreal and the Alleged Fraudulent Practice of Employment Agencies. Report of Commissioner and Evidence.* Ottawa: S.E. Dawson, Printer to the King, 1905. 173pp.

Canada. Department of Secretary of State. *Italians in Canada.* Ottawa: Canadian Citizenship Branch, Department of Secretary of State, 1949. 36pp.

Canada. Ministry of the Interior. *Immigration Facts and Figures.* Ottawa: Queen's Printer, 1913. 32pp.

Canada. Multiculturalism Directorate, Department of Secretary of State. *The Canadian Family Tree: Canada's*

Peoples. Ottawa: Queen's Printer, 1967; reprint ed., 1979. Section on Italians, pp. 128-33.

Canada. *Royal Commission on Canada's Economic Prospects, The Canadian Construction Industry*. Ottawa, 1956.

Canadian Encyclopedia, 1985. S.v. "Italians," by Franc Sturino. In Vol. 2, pp. 908-09.

Capacci, A. "I problemi connessi con la presenza dei lavoratori stranieri nell'Europa occidentale e nel Canada." *Bollettino della Società Geografica Italiana* Series X, 9 (1980): 549-52.

Cappadocia, Ezio. "Immigration: Old and New." *Italian Canadiana* 3, no. 1 (Spring 1987): 46-53.

Caraci, G. "La 'Vinland Map' " *Studi Medievali* 7 (1966): 509-15.

Careless, J.M.S. *Toronto: An Illustrated History to 1918*. The History of Canadian Cities Series. Toronto: James Lorimer and National Museum of Man, National Museums of Canada, 1984, pp. 157-59.

Casorso, Victor. *The Casorso Story: An account of 100 years of Social Life in the Okanagan Valley*. Okanagan Falls, B.C.: Rima Books, 1983. 192pp.

Cavalieri, Enea. "Il dominion del Canada. Appunti di Viaggio." *Nuova Antologia* (16 February, 16 March, 16 April 1879). Also published in *In giro per il mondo: Osservazioni e appunti*. Bologna, 1880.

Celli, Anna. "Italian Time Line." *Polyphony* 9, no. 1 (Fall/Winter 1987): 44-45. Re Sudbury, Ontario.

Cellini, Leo. "Emigration, the Italian Family, and Changing Roles." In *The Italian Immigrant Woman in North*

America. Edited by Betty Boyd Caroli, Robert F. Harney and Lydio F. Tomasi. Toronto: MHSO, 1978, pp. 273-87.

Ciano, C. "Terranova e Livorno nel secolo XVII." *Atti del III Convegno di Studi Colombiani.* Genoa, 1979, pp. 499-505.

Codignola, Luca. "L'America del Nord nei documenti dell'archivio della Sacra Congregazione 'De Propaganda Fide,' 1622-1799: Una introduzione, 1622-1799." In *Canadiana.* Vol. 2: *Storia e storiografia canadese,* pp. 33-45. Edited by Luca Codignola. Venice: Marsilio, 1979.

Codignola, Luca. "Notizie dal Nuovo Mondo. Propaganda Fide e il Nord America, 1622-1630." In *Canadiana.* Vol. 3: *Problemi di storia canadese,* pp. 32-44. Edited by Luca Codignola. Venice: Marsilio, 1983.

Codignola, Luca. *Terre d'America e burocrazia romana. Simon Stock, Propaganda Fide e la colonia di Lord Baltimore a Terranova, 1621-1649.* Venice: Marsilio, 1982.

Cometti, Elizabeth. "Trends in Italian Emigration." *Western Political Quarterly* 11 (December 1958): 820-34.

Community Resource Centre [of Windsor]. *Organizing for Workers' Power: Beyond Trade Unionism and Vanguardism.* Contains reprint of article by Adriano Sofri from *Les Temps Modernes,* October 1969. 19pp. Typescript.

Corazza, Gian Carlo, and Tabarroni, Giorgio. "Marconi e il Canada: passato e futuro." *Il Veltro* 1-2, anno XXIX (January-April 1985): 171-80.

Corbett, David C. *Canada's Immigration Policy: A Critique.* Toronto: University of Toronto Press, 1957. 215pp.

Cozzolino, Thomas. "Tramping and Contracting: An Italian Gang Boss of 1901." In *The Canadian Worker in the*

Twentieth Century, pp. 6-10. Edited by Irving Abella and David Miller. Toronto: Oxford University Press, 1978.

Cro, Stelio. "Padre Francesco Giuseppe Bressani (1612-1672) fra apologia e storia." In *Scritti sulla Nouvelle-France nel Seicento*. Quaderni Del Seicento Francese no. 6, pp. 141-55. Edited by P.A. Jannini, G. Dotoli and P. Carile. Bari: Adriatica, and Paris: Nizet, 1984.

Cro, Stelio. "Il primo missionario Italiano in Canada: Padre Francesco Giuseppe Bressani (1612-1672)." *Il Veltro* 1-2, anno XXIX (January-April 1985): 127-36.

Cumbo, Enrico. "Italians in Hamilton, 1900-40." *Polyphony* 7, no. 2 (Fall/Winter 1985): 28-36.

Cyriax, Tony. *Among Italian Peasants*. London: W. Collins Sons, 1919, pp. 232, 262.

D'Appolloni, Luigi. "Tels sont les Italo-Canadiens." *Relations* 10, no. 109 (February 1950): 36-40.

"Data on the Vital Statistics of Italians in Canada, 1934 and 1935." *Notiziario demografico* 11, no. 2 (February 1938): 33-35.

Davie, Maurice R. *World Immigration, with Special Reference to the United States*. New York, 1949. Chap. on Canada, pp. 416-26.

Davies, Adriana Albi. *Italians Settle In Edmonton*. Edmonton: Edmonton Historical Society, 1983. 22pp.

Dawson, S.E. "The Voyages of the Cabots." *Transactions of the Royal Society of Canada* 3, no. 2 (1897).

De Leone, Enrico. "Appunti per una storia dell'emigrazione italiana. L'emigrazione italiana in Canada nei primi decenni di questo secolo." *Immigration, Migration and Ethnic Groups in Canada*. Ottawa, 1969, pp. 43-45.

Del Negro, Piero. "Il Canada nella cultura veneziana del Settecento." In *Canadiana*. Vol. 3: *Storia e Storiografia canadese*, pp. 47-66. Edited by Luca Codignola. Venice: Marsilio, 1979.

Del Negro, Piero. "Le relazioni storiche tra l'italia e il Canada nell' eta moderna." *Il Veltro* 1-2, anno XXIX (January-April 1985): 53-71.

De Stefani, Carlo. *Il Canada e l'emigrazione italiana*. Florence; Tipografia Ricci, 1914.

Di Giacomo, James Louis. *They Live in the Moneta: An Overview of the History and Changes in Social Organization of Italians in Timmins, Ontario*. York Timmins Project, Working Paper no. 2. North York, Ontario: Institute for Behavioural Research, York University, 1982. 67 leaves. (Abridged version in *Polyphony* 7, no. 2 [Fall/Winter 1985]: 81-90.)

Di Stasi, Michael. *My Fifty Years of Italian Evangelism, 1905-1955: The Story of St. Paul's Italian United Church*. Toronto: St. Paul's Italian United Church, 1955. 40pp.

Douglass, William A. *Emigration in a South Italian Town: An Anthropological History*. New Brunswick, New Jersey: Rutgers University Press, 1984, pp. 2, 96-98, 114, 149, 186, 194-95, 205.

Duliani, Mario. *La Ville Sans Femme*. Montreal: Editions Pascal, 1945. 316pp.

Elliott, Jean Leonard. "Canadian Immigration: A Historical Assessment." In *Two Nations, Many Cultures: Ethnic*

Groups in Canada, pp. 160-72. Edited by Jean Leonard Elliott. Scarborough, Ontario: Prentice-Hall, 1979.

"Emigration During the Past Fifty Years." In *Italian Affairs* 3 (November 1954): 581-86. Updates for 1955 (in Vol. 5) and 1956 (in Vol. 7).

"Emigrazione Italiana in Canada." *Bollettino Quadriennale Dell' Emigrazione* 10, nos. 16-17 (September 1955): 239.

Encyclopedia Canadiana. 1962 ed. S.v. "Italian Origin, People of." In Vol. 5, pp. 332-34.

Encyclopedia Canadiana. 1966 ed. S.v. "Italian Origin, People of," by Merle Storey. In Vol. 5, pp. 332-34.

Evans, A. Margaret. "The Italians in Canada." In *On Italy and the Italians*, pp. 17-39. Edited by Gianni Bartocci. Guelph, Ontario: Office of Continuing Education, University of Guelph, 1974.

Farnocchia, Franca. "Italiani in Canada: il caso di Montréal." *Bollettino della Società Geografica Italiana* Series X, 10 (1981): 543-73.

Favero, Luigi, and Tassello, Graziano. "Cent' anni di emigrazione italiana (1876-1976)." In *Un secolo di emigrazione italiana: 1876-1976*, pp. 9-64. Edited by Gianfausto Rosoli. Rome: Centro Studi Emigrazione, 1978.

Foerster, Robert F. *The Italian Emigration of Our Times.* Cambridge: Harvard University Press, 1924; reprint ed., New York: Arno Press and the New York Times, 1969, pp. 17, 19, 31, 32, 320, 338, 345, 350-51, 359, 400.

Fortier, D'Iberville. "I rapporti tra l'Italia e il Canada." In *Canadiana*. Vol. 1: *Aspetti della storia e della litteratura canadese*, pp. 11-19. Edited by Luca Codignola. Venice: Marsilio Editori, 1978.

Frino-Zanovello, S. "La Relazione sulla Nuova Francia di Francesco Bressani." *Miscellanea di storia delle esplorazioni* 2 (1977): 105-18.

Giancana, Frank [pseud.] "Letter to a Politician." In *Working in Canada*, pp. 131-32. Edited by Walter Johnson. Montreal: Black Rose Books, 1975; 2nd revised ed., 1983.

Gianelli, A. "Sulle presenti condizioni del Canada. Rapporto." *Bollettino Consolare* (August 1872).

Gibbon, John Murray. *Canadian Mosaic: The Making of a Northern Nation*. Toronto: McClelland and Stewart, 1938. Italians, pp. 380-93.

Gibbon, John Murray. "The Foreign Born." *Queen's Quarterly* 27, no. 4 (April-June 1920): 331-51.

Giunta Cattolica Italiana per l'Emigrazione. *Canada. Note di orientamento*. Rome, 1961. 52 pp.

Giuliani-Balestrino, M.C. "L'emigrazione italiana in America." *Il Veltro* 3-4, anno XXXI (May-August 1987): 301-26.

Giunta, F. "Contributo italiano al chiarimento della questione di Vinlandia." *Atti del I Convegno Internazionale di Studi Colombiani*. Genoa, 1974, pp. 93-110.

Goggio, Emilio. "Italian influences on the cultural life of old Montreal." *Canadian Modern Language Review* 9, no. 1 (Fall 1952), pp. 5-7.

Gualtieri, Francesco M. *We Italians: A Study in Italian Immigration in Canada*. Toronto: Italian World War Veterans' Association, 1928. 77pp.

Hardwick, Francis C., ed. *From an Antique Land: Italians in Canada*. Canadian Culture Series no. 6. Vancouver: Tantalus Research, 1976. 88pp.

Harney, Robert F. "Ambiente and Social Class in North American Little Italies." *Canadian Review of Studies in Nationalism* 2, no. 2 (Spring 1975): 208-24.

Harney, Robert F. "Boarding and Belonging: Thoughts on Sojourner Institutions." *Urban History Review*, no. 2-78 (October 1978): 28-37.

Harney, Robert F. "Chiaroscuro: Italians in Toronto, 1885-1915." *Italian Americana* 1, no. 2 (Spring 1975): 143-67. (Abridged version in *Polyphony* 6, no. 1 [Spring/Summer 1984]: 44-49.)

Harney, Robert F. "The Commerce of Migration." *Canadian Ethnic Studies* 9, no. 1 (1977): 42-53.

Harney, Robert F. *Dalla Frontiera alle Little Italies: Gli italiani in Canada*. Rome: Bonacci Editore, 1984. 313pp.

Harney, Robert F. "How to Write a History of Postwar Toronto Italia." *Polyphony* 7, no. 2 (Fall/Winter 1985): 61-65.

Harney, Robert F. "The Italian Community in Toronto." In *Two Nations, Many Cultures*, pp. 220-36. Edited by Jean Leonard Elliott. Toronto: Prentice-Hall, 1979.

Harney, Robert F. "Italians in Canada." In *The Culture of Italy: Mediaeval to Modern*, pp. 225-46. Edited by S. Bernard Chandler and Julius A. Molinaro. Toronto: Griffin House, 1979.

Harney, Robert F. *Italians in North America*. Toronto: MHSO, n.d. 45 pp. (Revised ed. of *Italians in Canada*. Occasional Papers on Ethnic and Immigration Studies, O.P. 78-1. Toronto: MHSO, 1978.)

Harney, Robert F. "Italophobia: English-speaking malady?" *Studi Emigrazione/Etudes Migrations* no. 77 (March 1985): 6-43. (Abridged version in *Polyphony* 7, no. 2 [Fall/Winter 1985]: 54-59.)

Harney, Robert F. "Men Without Women: Italian Migrants in Canada, 1885-1930." In *The Italian Immigrant Woman in North America*, pp. 79-101. Edited by Betty Boyd Caroli, Robert F. Harney and Lydio F. Tomasi. Toronto: MHSO, 1978. (Reprinted in *Canadian Ethnic Studies* 11, no. 1 [1979], pp. 29-47.)

Harney, Robert F. "Montreal's King of Italian Labour: A Case Study of Padronism." *Labour/Le Travailleur* 4, no. 4 (1979): 57-84.

Harney, Robert F. "The History of Italians in Toronto." Paper presented at the First Annual Elia Lecture Series in Italian-Canadian Studies, York University, North York, Ontario, 2 February 1984. 58 leaves.

Harney, Robert F. "The Padrone and the Immigrant." *Canadian Review of American Studies* 5, no. 2 (Fall 1974): 101-18.

Harney, Robert F. "The Padrone System and Sojourners in the Canadian North, 1885-1920." In *Pane e Lavoro: The Italian American Working Class*, pp. 119-37. Edited by George E. Pozzetta. Toronto: MHSO, 1980

Harney, Robert F. *Toronto: Canada's New Cosmopolite.* Occasional Papers in Ethnic and Immigration Studies, O.P. 81-11. Toronto: MHSO, 1978. 22pp. (Abridged version in *Canadian Geographic Journal* [April/May 1978].)

Harney, Robert F. "Toronto's Little Italy, 1885-1945." In *Little Italies in North America*, pp. 41-61. Edited by Robert F. Harney and J. Vincenza Scarpaci. Toronto: MHSO, 1981.

Harney, Robert F. "Uomini senza donne. Emigrati italiani in Canada, 1885-1930." In *Canadiana*. Vol. 2: *Storia e Storiografia canadese*, pp. 67-95. Edited by Luca Codignola. Venice: Marsilio Editori, 1979.

Harney, Robert F., and Troper, Harold. *Immigrants: a Portrait of the Urban Experience, 1890-1930*. Toronto: Van Nostrand Reinhold, 1975. 212pp.

Hastings, J.C.O. *Report of the Toronto Medical Health Officer Dealing with the Recent Investigation of Slum Conditions in Toronto. Embodying Recommendations for the Amelioration of the Same*. Toronto, 1911.

Hawkins, Freda. *Canada and Immigration: Public Policy and Public Concern*. Montreal: McGill-Queen's Press, 1972. 444pp.

Hudak, Ladislas. "The Italians in Canada." Report prepared by the Ethnic Press Analysis Section, Canadian Citizenship Branch, Department of the Secretary of State, Ottawa, 1967. 51 leaves.

Hurd, W. Burton. "The Case for a Quota." *Queen's Quarterly* 36 (Winter 1929): 145-59.

Hurd, W. Burton. *1941: Ethnic Origin and Nativity of the Canadian People*. Ottawa: Minister of Trade and Commerce, 1943.

Iacovetta, Franca. "From 'Contadina' to Worker: Southern Italian Immigrant Working Women in Toronto, 1947-62." In *Looking into My Sister's Eyes: an Exploration in Women's History*, pp. 195-222. Edited by Jean Burnet. Toronto: MHSO, 1986. (Abridged version in *Polyphony* 7, no. 2 [Fall/Winter, 1985]: 91-97.)

Imperatori, Ugo E. *Dizionario di italiani all estero (dal secolo XIII sino ad oggi)*. Genoa: L'Emigrante, 1956. 365pp.

"Italian Communities Abroad." *International Migration* 8, no. 3 (1970): 121-29.

"Italian Emigration during the Period from 1946 to 1954." *Italian Affairs* 4 (November 1955): 985-95.

"Italian Immigration in 1952 and 1953." *Industry and Labour* 13 (May 1955): 460-64.

Italian Information Bureau. *Annuario Italiano*, editions 1930 to 1935. (1929-30 edition titled *Italian City Directory*.) 1935 ed., 112pp.

"Italian Migration." *Research Digest* 11, no. 4 (1960): 96pp. Published by Geneva-based Intergovernmental Committee for European Migration.

"Italian Migration in 1957." *Industry and Labour* 21 (March 1959): 213-19.

Italiani nel Mondo. *Il lavoratore italiano in Canada*. Rome: Direzione Generale Dell' Emigrazione and Affari Sociali del Ministero degli Affari Esteri, 1966. 95pp. 1969 ed., 112pp.

"Italians Work Canadian Farms, Grow Sugar Beets." *Up and Down the Rows*, no. 107 (Winter 1955): 6.

Italy. Commissariato Generale dell' Emigrazione. *Annuario statistico sull' emigrazione negli anni 1869-1875*. Pt. 2 includes Canada.

Italy. Commissariato Generale dell' Emigrazione. *L'Emigrazione italiana dal 1910 al 1923*. Rome, 1926. Vol. 2, pt. 1 on Canada. Update published same year for 1924-25. Pt. 3 on Canada.

Italy. Direzione Generale delle Opere di Emigrazione. *Indirizzi delle Missioni e delle Parrocchie per l'assistenza degli italiani emigrati.* Rome, 1963. Sec. on Canada.

Itroc [pseud.]. "Can an Italian-Canadian Be a Fascist?" *Polyphony* 7, no. 2 (Fall/Winter 1985): 52-53. Translation of article bv Harry Corti from *l'Emigrato*, 30 March 1932.

Kubat, Daniel. "Canada." In *The Politics of Migration Policies*, pp. 19-36. Edited by Daniel Kubat. New York: Center for Migration Studies, 1979.

Kuitunen, Maddalena. "Il Canadà, l'educazione dell' emigrante e la 'Rivista Coloniale' (1906-1911)." *Italian Canadiana* 3, no. 1 (Spring 1987): 34-45.

Kuitunen, Maddalena. "Italian and Italians in the Academic Institutions of English-Speaking Canada (1840-1887)." *Italian Canadiana* 2, no. 1 (Spring 1986): 1-13.

Kuitunen, Maddalena. "L'italianistica e l'emigrazione italiana a Toronto (1853-1984)." *Italian Canadiana* 1, no. 1 (Spring 1985): 38-50.

Landra, Angelo. "La colonizzazione del Canada e l'emigrazione italiana." *Gazzetta Coloniale* (1907).

Lauriente, Camille. *The Chronicles of Camille.* New York: Pageant Press, 1953, pp. 86-103.

LaVigna, Claire. "Women in the Canadian and Italian Trade Union Movements at the Turn of the Century: A Comparison." In *The Italian Immigrant Woman in North America*, pp. 32-42. Edited by Betty Boyd Caroli, Robert F. Harney and Lydio Tomasi. Toronto: MHSO, 1978.

Lee, Egmont. "Studiosi Canadesi di storia Italiana." *Il Veltro* 1-2, anno XXIX (January-April 1985): 197-203.

Lemon, James. *Toronto: An Illustrated History since 1918*. The History of Canadian Cities Series. Toronto: James Lorimer and National Museum of Man, National Museums of Canada, 1985, pp. 51, 113, 125, 174, 176, 196.

Lodolini, Elio. "I volontari del Canada nell'esercito pontifico (1868-1870)." *Rassegna Storica del Risorgimento* 56, no. 4 (1969): 641-87.

Losina, Costantino. "Gli italiani nella provincia dell' Ontario." *Bollettino della Reale Società Geografico Italiana* 4 (1927): 19-32.

Lucas, Frederick William. *Annals of the Voyages of the Brothers Nicolo and Antonio Zeno in the North Atlantic About the End of the XIV C*. London: Stevens Son and Stiles, 1898.

Lucrezio, Giuseppe M. "A Century of Italian Emigration." *Migration News* 10 (March-April 1961): 1-4.

Lucrezio, Giuseppe M. and Favero, Luigi. "Un quarto di secolo di emigrazione italiana." *Studi Emigrazione/Etudes Migrations* no. 25-26 (March-June 1972): 31-58.

Manzi, E. "La nuova immigrazione come fatto determinante nella geografia umana del Canada." *La Geografia nelle Scuole* 20 (1975): 18-30.

Martin, John D.P. "The Regiment De Watteville: Its Settlement and Service in Upper Canada." *Ontario History* 52, no. 1 (March 1960): 17-29.

Massicotte, Z. "L'orgue de Barbarie." *Bulletin des Recherches Historiques* 50, no. 4 (April 1944): 117-19.

Menchini, Camillo. "Il Canada di Jacques Cartier e di Giovanni da Verrazzano." *Il Veltro* 1-2, anno XXIX (January-April 1985): 115-25.

Menchini, Camillo. *Francesco Giuseppe Bressani*. Primo missionario italiano in Canada. Montreal: Edizioni Insieme, 1980. 169pp. Also available in French.

Menchini, Camillo. *Giovanni Caboto: scopritore del Canada*. Montreal: Edizioni Riviera, 1974. 191pp.

Merlino, S. "Italian Immigrants and Their Enslavement." *The Forum*, April 1983, pp. 183-90.

"Migration to and from Italy in 1957, 1958 and 1959." *Industry and Labour* 25 (April 1961): 212-21.

Mingarelli, Giosafat. *Gli Italiani di Montreal: Note e Profili*, 2nd ed. Montreal: Centro Italiano attivita commerciali-artistiche, 1971. 282pp.

Molinaro, Julius A. "Albert Wyatt Reid and 'Il Mondo Libero': A Canadian in Rome (1944-1945)." *Italian Canadiana* 3, no. 1 (Spring 1987): 1-33.

Molinaro, Julius A. "Due pionieri della cultura Italiana in Canada: Giacomo Forneri e Emilio Goggio." *Il Veltro* 1-2, anno XXIX (January-April 1985): 211-18.

Molinaro, Julius A. "Edoardo Ferrari-Fontana: An Italian Contribution to Music in Ontario." *Italian Canadiana* 1, no. 1 (Spring 1985): 1-11.

Moncarz, Raul. "Italian Communities Abroad." *International Migration* 8, no. 3 (1970): 121-29.

Moncarz, Raul. "Italian Emigration."*International Migration* 8, no. 3 (1970): 117-20.

Monticelli, Giuseppe Lucrezio. "A Century of Italian Emigration." *Migration News* no. 2 (March-April 1961): 1-4.

Moroni Parken, Anna. *Emigranti: quattro anni al Canadà*. Milan: Solmi, 1907. 143pp.

Morrison, Jean. "Ethnicity and Class Consciousness: British, Finnish and South European Workers at the Canadian Lakehead before World War I." *Lakehead University Review* (1976): 41-54.

Morrison, Jean. "Ethnicity and Violence: The Lakehead Freight Handlers Before World War I." In *Essays in Canadian Working Class History*, pp. 143-60. Edited by Gregory S. Kealey and Peter Warrian. Toronto: McClelland and Stewart, 1976; reprint ed., 1979.

Negri, Cristoforo. "Le navigazioni alla Nuova-Brunswick." In *La Grandezza Italiana. Studi, confronti, desideri*. Turin, 1864, p. 109.

Norris, John. *Strangers Entertained: A History of Ethnic Groups of British Columbia*. Vancouver: Evergreen Press and B.C. Centennial '71 Committee, 1971. Chap. 11.

Olgiati, Francesca. *Uomini piccoli e uomini grandi (G.B. de La Salle)*. Milan, 1921.

Ontario. Ministry of Labour. *Immigrant Women in the Labour Force*. 1975.

Ontario. *Royal Commission on Labor-Management Relations in the Construction Industry*. Toronto, 1962.

"Il padiglione del Canada." *Esposizione di Milano* 5 (October 1906): 146.

Painchaud, Claude, and Poulin, Richard. "Le phénomène migratoire italien et la formation de la communauté italo-quebécoise." Ottawa: Université d'Ottawa, 1981. 529 leaves. Typescript.

Palmer, Howard. *Land of Second Chance: A History of Ethnic Groups in Southern Alberta.* Lethbridge: Lethbridge Herald, 1972. Chap. 12, pp. 174-81.

Palmer, Howard. *Patterns of Prejudice: A History of Nativism in Alberta.* The Canadian Social History Series. Toronto: McClelland & Stewart, 1982, pp. 27, 76, 133, 165-67.

Palmer, Howard, ed. *Immigration and the Rise of Multiculturalism.* Toronto: Copp Clark, 1975, pp. 76, 159. Reprint of articles from *La Comunità* (Montreal), 1970 and 1971.

Parkman, Francis. *The Discovery of the Great West: "La Salle."* Edited by William R. Taylor. New York: Holt, Rinehart and Winston, 1956; reprint ed., 1965. Sections on Henri de Tonty. 354pp.

Pautasso, Luigi. "La Donna Italiana Durante il Periodo Fascista in Toronto 1930-1940." In *The Italian Immigrant Woman in North America*, pp. 168-86. Edited by Betty Boyd Caroli, Robert F. Harney, and Lydio Tomasi. Toronto: MHSO, 1978. (Also in *Quaderni canadesi* 1, no. 1 (1977), pp. 3-12.)

Pautasso, Luigi. "La propaganda fascista in Canada alla vigilia della guerra d'Etopia." *Quaderni canadesi* 2, no. 3 (March-April 1978): 15-16.

Peressini, Mauro. "Stratégies migratoires et pratiques communautaires: Les Italiens du Frioul." *Recherches sociographiques* 25, no. 3 (September-December 1984): 367-91.

Perin, Roberto. "Conflits d'identité et d'allegeance: la propagande du consulat italien à Montréal dans les années 1930." *Questions de Culture* 2 (1982): 81-102.

Perin, Roberto. "Making Good Fascists and Good Canadians: Consular Propaganda and the Italian Community in Montreal in the 1930s." In *Minorities and Mother Country Imagery*. Social and Economic Papers no. 13, pp. 136-58. Edited by Gerald L. Gold. St. John's, Newfoundland: Institute of Social and Economic Research, 1984.

Perin, Roberto. "I rapporti tra Italia e Canada nell' ottocento. *Il Veltro* 1-2, anno XXIX (January-April 1985): 73-90.

Perin, Roberto. "Religion, Ethnicity and Identity: Placing the Immigrant within the Church." In *Canadian Issues/ Themes Canadiens*. Vol. 7: *Religion/Culture: Comparative Canadian Studies*, pp. 212-29. Edited by William Westfall et al. Ottawa: Association for Canadian Studies, 1985.

Pisani, Pietro. *Il Canada presente e futuro in relazione all' emigrazione italiana*. Rome: Tipografia dell' Unione Cooperative Editrice, 1909. 171pp.

Porri, Vincenzo. "Il pericolo del Canada." *Vita Italiana all' estero* (April 1913): 303-06.

"Post-War Italian Overseas Migration." *Migration Facts and Figures* no. 10 (July-August 1957): 1-4.

Potestio, John. *The History of the Italian Mutual Benefit Society (1929-1984)*. Thunder Bay, Ontario: Lehto Printers, 1985. 128pp.

Potestio, John. "Le memorie di Giovanni Veltri: da contadino a impresario di ferrorie." *Studi Emigrazione/Etudes Migrations* no. 77 (March 1985): 129-40.

Potestio, John, ed. *The Memoirs of Giovanni Veltri*. Toronto: MHSO and Ontario Heritage Foundation, 1987. 76pp. (Abridged version in *Polyphony* 7, no. 2 [Fall/Winter 1985]: 14-19.)

Powell River, B.C., Golden Jubilee, 1910-1960. Powell River: Power River News [1960], unpaginated.

Principe, Angelo. "The Italo-Canadian Anti-Fascist Press in Toronto (1922-1940)." *Nemla Italian Studies* 4: *Proceedings: Italian Section, Northeast Modern Language Association Conference* (1980): 119-37. (Abridged version in *Polyphony* 7, no. 2 [Fall/Winter 1985]: 43-51.)

Principe, Angelo. "Il Risorgimento Visto dai Protestanti dell' Alto Canada: 1846-1860." *Rassegna Storica del Risorgimento* 66, no. 2 (1979): 151-63.

Principe, Angelo. "Upper Canadian Protestant Perception of the Italian 'Risorgimento': 1845-1860." *Papers of the Canadian Society of Church History.* 1976.

Pucci, Antonio. "At the Forefront of Militancy: Italians in Canada at the Turn of the 20th Century." *Studi Emigrazione/Etudes Migrations* no. 77 (March 1985): 112-28. (Abridged version in *Polyphony* 7, no. 2 [Fall/Winter 1985]: 37-42.)

Pucci, Antonio. "Canadian Industrialization versus the Italian 'Contadini' in a Decade of Brutality, 1902-1912." In *Little Italies in North America*, pp. 183-207. Edited by Robert F. Harney and J. Vincenza Scarpaci. Toronto: MHSO, 1981.

Pucci, Antonio. "Community in the Making: A Case Study of a Benevolent Society in Fort William's 'Little Italy'." *Thunder Bay Historical Museum Society, Papers and Records* 6 (1978): 16-27.

Pucci, Antonio. "The Società Italiana Di Benevolenza – Principe De Piemonte." *Polyphony* 2, no. 1 (Winter 1979): 19-25.

Pucci, Antonio. "Thunder Bay's Two Little Italies: 1880s-1940s." *Polyphony* 9, no. 2 (1987): 51-59.

Ramirez, Bruno. "Brief Encounters: Italian Immigrant Workers and the CPR, Montreal 1900-1930." Paper presented at Elia Chair Seminar Series in Italian-Canadian Studies, YorkUniversity, North York, Ontario, 12 March 1986. 22 leaves.

Ramirez, Bruno. "Brief Encounters: Italian Immigrant Workers and the CPR, 1900-30." *Labour/Le Travail* 17 (Spring 1986): 9-27.

Ramirez, Bruno. "Italian Roots." *Horizon Canada* 1, no. 7 (March 1985): 164-68. Also available in French.

Ramirez, Bruno. "Montreal's Italians and the Socioeconomy of Settlement 1900-1930: Some Historical Hypotheses." *Urban History Review* 10, no. 1 (June 1981): 39-48.

Ramirez, Bruno. "Operai senza una 'causa'? I manoroli italiani a Montreal, 1900-1930." *Studi Emigrazione/Etudes Migrations* no. 77 (March 1985): 98-111.

Ramirez, Bruno. *Les Premiers Italiens de Montréal: L'Origine de la Petite Italie du Québec*. Montreal: Boréal Express, 1984.136pp.

Ramirez, Bruno, and Del Balso, Michael. *The Italians of Montreal: From Sojourning to Settlement, 1900-1921*. Montreal: Editions du Courant, 1980. 54pp.

Razzolini, Esperanza Maria. *All Our Fathers: The North Italian Colony in Industrial Cape Breton*. Ethnic Heritage Series Vol.8. Halifax: International Education Centre, Saint Mary's University, 1983. 55pp.

Rebecca, Domenico. "Lettere dal Canada." *L'Esplorazione Commerciale. Giornale di viaggi e di geografia commerciale*. 1901, pp. 273-76.

Restaldi, Vittorio V. "Memoriale sugli Italiani nei campi di internamento (1940-1942)." *Quaderni canadesi* 2, no. 2 (January-February 1978): 5-8.

Ribordy, François-Xavier. "Conflit de culture et criminalité des Italiens à Montréal." *Studi Emigrazione/Etudes Migrations* no. 28 (1972): 453-54.

Rolle, Andrew F. *The Immigrant Upraised: Italian Adventurers and Colonists in an Expanding America.* Norman, Oklahoma: University of Oklahoma Press, 1968. Section on Western Canada, pp. 219-22.

Rosoli, Gianfausto, ed. *Un secolo di emigrazione italiana: 1876-1976.* Rome: Centro Studi Emigrazione, 1978. Appendix, Tables 3 and 6.

Sabia, Laura. " 'You Are Not One of Us': The Roots of My Militant Feminism." *Canadian Women Studies/les cahiers de la femme* 8, no. 2 (Summer 1987): 32-36.

Sacchetti, G. Battista. "L'atteggiamento del Canada francese nei riguardi dell'immigrazione." *Studi Emigrazione/ Etudes Migrations* no. 8 (1967): 97-122.

Sanfilippo, Matteo. "Le famiglie Tonti e Di Lietto nella Nuova Francia." *Il Veltro* 1-2, anno XXIX (January-April 1985): 151-55.

Savard, Pierre. "L'Italia nella cultura franco-canadese dell' Ottocento." In *Canadiana.* Vol. 3: *Problemi di storia canadese*, pp. 91-106. Edited by Luca Codignola. Venice: Marsilio, 1983.

Saverio, Fino. *S. Giovanni Battista de La Salle.* Turin, 1929.

Scardellato, Gabriel P. "Italian Immigrant Workers in Powell River, B.C.: A Case Study of Settlement Before World War II." *Labour/Le Travail* 16 (Fall 1985): 145-63.

Scardellato, Gabriel P. "Lavoratori tempora nei ... nell' America Canadese." *Il Veltro* (April 1984).

Scarpaci, Vincenza J. "La Contadina: The Plaything of the Middle Class Woman Historian." *Journal of Ethnic Studies* 9, no. 2 (1981): 21-38.

Scott, Stanley. "A Profusion of Issues: Immigrant Labour, the World War, and the Cominco Strike of 1917." *Labour/Le Travailleur* 2: 54-78.

Scott, W.D. "Immigration and Population." In *Canada and Its Provinces* 7, pp. 561-63. Edited by A. Shortt and A. Doughty. Toronto: Brook, 1914.

Smith, William George. *A Study in Canadian Immigration.* Toronto: Ryerson Press, 1920. 397pp.

Solimbergo, Giuseppe. "Il Canada sotto l'aspetto economico e politico. Rapporto del Comm. Giuseppe Solimbergo, R. Console Generale in Montreal." *Bollettino del Ministero degli Affari Esteri* no. 190 (March 1901): 169-205. Also in same volume, "Emigrazione al Canadà," pp. 277-78.

Spada, A.V. *The Italians in Canada.* Ottawa: Riviera Publishers, 1969. 387pp.

Stephenson, F.C. "Mission Work among Italians in Canada." In *Religious Work among Italians in America: A Survey for the Home Missions Council,* pp. 38-39. Edited by Antonio Mangano. Philadelphia: Board of the Home Missions and Church Extension of the Methodist Episcopal Church, 1917; reprinted in *Protestant Evangelism among Italians in America.* Edited by Francesco Cordasco. New York: Arno Press and the New York Times, 1975.

Sturino, Franc. "A Case Study of Immigrant Mobility in Toronto, 1930-1967." In *Records of the Past: Exploring*

New Sources in Social History, pp. 35-68. Edited by Edward Jackson and Ian Winchester. Toronto: Ontario Institute for Studies in Education, 1979.

Sturino, Franc. "A Case Study of a South Italian Family in Toronto, 1934-1960." *Urban History Review* no. 2-78 (1978): 38-57.

Sturino, Franc. "Contours of Postwar Italian Immigration to Toronto." *Polyphony* 6, no. 1 (Spring/Summer 1984): 127-30.

Sturino, Franc. "Italian Immigration to Canada and the Farm Labour System through the 1920's." *Studi Emigrazione/ Etudes Migrations* no. 77 (March 1985): 81-97.

Sturino, Franc. "Post-War Italian Immigration to Toronto." Paper presented at the First Annual Elia Chair Lecture Series in Italian-Canadian Studies, York University, North York, Ontario, 16 February 1984. 42 leaves.

Sturino, Franc. "Post-World War Two Canadian Immigration Policy towards Italians." *Polyphony* 7, no. 2 (Fall/Winter 1985): 67-72.

Sturino, Franc. "The Role of Women in Italian Immigration to the New World." In *Looking into My Sister's Eyes: an Exploration in Women's History*, pp. 21-32. Edited by Jean Burnet. Toronto: MHSO, 1986. (Abridged version in *Polyphony* 8, no. 1-2 [1986]: 21-23.)

Sturino, Franc, and Zucchi, John E., eds. *Italians in Ontario.* Special issue of *Polyphony* 7, no. 2 (Fall/Winter 1985). 147pp.

Sylvain, Robert. *Clerc, Garibaldien Predicant des Deux Mondes. Alessandro Gavazzi (1809-1889).* 2 vols. Quebec: Le Centre Pédagogique, Place de L'Institut Canadien, 1962. 441pp.

Sylvain, Robert. "Sejour mouvementé d'un Revolutionnaire
Italien à Toronto et à Québec." *Revue d'Historie de
l'Amerique Française* 13, no. 2 (September 1959): 183-229.

Taddeo, Donat J. and Taras, Raymond. *The Language of
Education Debate: A Study of the Political Dynamics
Between Quebec's Education Authorities and the Italian
Community.* Montreal: McGill-Queen's University Press,
1983.

Tedeschi, Mario. *Le prospettive dell' emigrazione italiana.*
Rome: O.E.T. Edizioni del Secolo, [1946]. 252pp. Pt. 2 on
Canada.

Temelini, Walter. "The Italians in Windsor." *Polyphony* 7, no.
2 (Fall/Winter 1985): 73-80.

Temelini, Walter. "Study of an Agricultural Community: The
Italians of Leamington." *Italian Canadiana* 3, no. 1
(Spring 1987): 80-91.

Timlin, Mabel F. "Canada's Immigration Policy, 1896-1910."
The Canadian Journal of Economics and Political Science
26, no. 4 (November 1960): 517-32.

The Torontonians: Toronto's Multicultural Heritage. Toronto:
Toronto Historical Board, 1982. Section, "The Italians,"
pp. 18-19.

Trudel, Marcel. "In Search of Asia." *Horizon Canada* 1, no. 2
(October 1984): 25-31. Also available in French.

Vangelisti, Guglielmo M. *Gli Italiani in Canada.* Montreal:
Chiesa Italiana di N.S. Della Difesa; revised ed., 1958.
330pp.

Verna, Anthony. "I nomi d'origine Italiana nella toponomastica Canadese." *Il Veltro* 3-4, anno XXIX (May-August 1985): 495-502.

Villata, Bruno. "Piemontesi nella nuova Francia con il reggimento 'Carignano'." *Il Veltro* 1-2, anno XXIX (January-April 1985): 137-50.

Visentin, Maurizio A. "The Italians of Sudbury." *Polyphony* 5, no. 1 (Spring/Summer 1983): 30-36.

Wallace, William Stewart. "The Story of Charlotte and Cornelia De Grassi." *Royal Society of Canada Transactions* 35 (1941).

Weare, George Edward. *Cabot's Discovery of North America.* London, 1918.

Williamson, J.A. *The Cabot Voyage and Bristol Discovery under Henry VII.* Cambridge, 1972.

Woodsworth, James A. *Strangers Within Our Gates: Or Coming Canadians.* Toronto: Young People's Forward Movement Department of the Methodist Church, 1909; reprint ed., Toronto: University of Toronto Press, 1972, Italians, pp. 131-35.

Workers Solidarity Committee and Community Resource Centre, Windsor. *For Canadian Workers: Lessons from Italy.* (Also published as *Italy, New Tactics and Organization.*) Pamphlet Vol. 1, no. 1. Windsor, Ontario, [1971]. 31pp.

Zavatti, S. "Il genovese Germano Eynard missionario nel nord-ovest canadese." *Miscellanea di storia delle esplorazioni* 3 (1978): 203-22.

Zavatti, S. "Un rarissimo opuscolo genovese reguardante gli Eschimesi." *Miscellanea di storia delle esplorazione* 1 (1975): 197-211.

Zucchi, John E. "The Annuario Italiano: A Toronto Italian City Directory." *Polyphony* 3, no. 1 (Winter 1981): 31-33.

Zucchi, John E. "Church, Clergy, and the Religious Life of Toronto's Italian Immigrants, 1900-1940." In *Proceedings of the Fiftieth Anniversary Conference of the Canadian Catholic Historical Association*. Ottawa, 1984, pp. 533-48.

Zucchi, John E. "Gli Italiani in Ontario prima della guerra 1915-18." *Il Veltro* 1-2, anno XXIX (January-April 1985): 157-70.

Zucchi, John E. "Italian Hometown Settlements and the Development of an Italian Community in Toronto, 1875-1935." In *Gathering Place: Peoples and Neighbourhoods of Toronto, 1834-1935*. Studies in Ethnic and Immigration History, pp. 121-46. Edited by Robert F. Harney. Toronto: MHSO, 1985. (Abridged version in *Polyphony* 7, no. 2 [Fall/Winter 1985]: 20-27.)

Zucchi, John E. *The Italian Immigrants of the St. John's Ward, 1875-1915: Patterns of Settlement and Neighbourhood Formation*. Occasional Papers in Ethnic and Immigration Studies, O.P. 81-10. Toronto: MHSO, 1981. 43pp.

Zucchi, John E. "Mining, Railway Building and Street Construction: Italians in Ontario before World War One." *Polyphony* 7, no. 2 (Fall/Winter 1985): 7-13.

Zucchi, John E. "Occupations, Enterprise and Migration Chain: the Fruit Traders from Termini Imerese in Toronto, 1900-1930." *Studi Emigrazione/Etudes Migrations* no. 77 (March 1985): 68-80.

Zucchi, John E. "Occupazioni, iniziative commerciali e catena migratoria: i commercianti di frutta da Termini Imerese a Toronto, 9400-1930." *Nuovi Quaderni del Meridione* 24, no. 95-96 (1986): 233-45.

Zucchi, John E. "Paesani or Italiani? Local and National Loyalties in an Italian Immigrant Community." In *The Family and Community Life of Italian Americans*, pp. 147-60. Edited by Richard N. Juliani. Staten Island, New York: American-Italian Historical Association, 1983.

Zucchi, John E. "Precursors of the 'New Immigration': Italian Street Musicians 1815-1885." Paper presented at the Elia Chair Seminar Series in Italian-Canadian Studies, York University, North York, Ontario, 13 February 1986. 20 leaves.

College and Robert Street, Toronto, 1984. Courtesy David Levine

SECTION 2:
SOCIAL AND CULTURAL LIFE

Alessio, Antonio. "Pirandello in Canada." *Il Veltro* 3-4, anno XXIX (May-August 1985): 403-13.

Almanacco 1987 dell' Italo-Canadese: Cronistoria degli avvenimenti del 1987: comunita, Canada, Italia, mondo e sport. Rexdale (Etobicoke), Ontario: Tor-Vis Promotions, 1987. 300pp. Third in a series.

Amprimoz, Alexandre L., and Viselli, Sante A. "Death Between Two Cultures: Italian-Canadian Poetry." In *Contrasts: Comparative Essays on Italian-Canadian Writing*, pp. 101-20. Edited by Joseph Pivato. Montreal: Guernica, 1985.

Amprimoz, Alexandre L., and Viselli, Sante A. "La generazione del silenzio: il movimento Caccia-D'Alfonso." *Italian Canadiana* 2, no. 1 (Spring 1986): 86-97.

Amprimoz, Alexandre L., and Viselli, Sante A. "Le jardinier qui roule ses 'r': littéraire au Québec." *Italian Canadiana* 3, no. 1 (Spring 1987): 68-79.

Anderson, Alan B., and Frideres, James S. *Ethnicity in Canada*. Toronto: Butterworths, 1981.

Ares, Richard. *Les positions ethniques, linguistiques et religieuses des Canadiens français a la suite du recensement de 1971*. Montreal: Bellarmin, 1975.

Augimeri, Maria C. *Calabrese Folklore*. Canadian Centre for Folk Culture Studies, Mercury Series Paper no. 56. Ottawa: National Museums of Canada, 1985. 255pp.

Augimeri, Maria C. *Italian Canadians: A Cross Section: A National Survey of Italian-Canadian Communities.* Ottawa: National Congress of Italian Canadians, 1978. 268pp.

Augimeri, Maria C. "View of Youth on Unity." In *Unity Within Diversity*, pp. 72-77. Edited by Shiu L. Kong and R. Ray. Toronto: University of Toronto Press, 1978.

Aversa, Alfred. "Italian New-Ethnicity: The Search for Self-Identity." *Journal of Ethnic Studies* 6, no. 2 (Summer 1978): 49-56.

Baldacci, Osvaldo. *L'incidenza geografico-culturale del gruppo etnico italiano nel contesto urbano di Toronto* . Rome: Libreria P. Tombolini, 1971. 43pp.

"Balestreri, Violet." In *Thirty-Four Biographies of Canadian Composers.* Montreal: CBC International Service, 1964, pp. 10-13.

Berry, John W., Kalin, Rudolf, and Taylor, Donald M. *Multiculturalism and Ethnic Attitudes in Canada.* Ottawa: Supply and Services Canada, 1977. 359pp.

Bianco, Carla, and Angiuli, Emanuela. *Emigrazione: Una recerca anthropologica de Carla Bianco sui pocessi de acculturazione relativi all'emigrazione italiana negli Stati Uniti, in Canada e in Italia.* Bari, Italy: Dedalo Libri, 1980. 189pp.

Billings, Robert. "Contemporary Influences on the Poetry of Mary di Michele." In *Contrasts: Comparative Essays on Italian-Canadian Writing*, pp. 121-52. Edited by Joseph Pivato. Montreal: Guernica, 1985.

Bitelli, Giovanni, and Foschi, Anna. *Emigrante: Storie, Memorie, Segreti della Buona Cucina dei Nostri Pionieri.*

Vancouver: Italian Senior Citizens Association and Centro Culturale Italiano, 1985. 112pp.

Boissevain, Jeremy. "Family and Kinship among Italians of Montreal." In *The Canadian Family*, revised ed., pp. 506-17. Edited by K. Ishwaran. Toronto: Holt, Rinehart and Winston, 1976.

Boissevain, Jeremy. *The Italians of Montreal: Social Adjustment in a Plural Society.* Studies of the Royal Commission on Bilingualism and Biculturalism no. 7. Ottawa: Information Canada, 1970. 87pp. Also available in French, 1971.

Bressan, Ottorino. *Non Dataci Lenticchie: Esperienze Commenti Prospettive di Vita Italo-Canadese.* Toronto: Gagliano Printing, [1962]. 150pp.

Caccia, Charles L. *Industrial English.* Toronto: By the Author, 1960. 112pp.

Caccia, Charles L. "Is Management Failing its New Canadian Employees?" *Industrial Canada* 60, no. 9 (February 1960): 43-44.

Caccia, Fulvio. "The Italian Writer and Language." In *Contrasts. Comparative Essays on Italian-Canadian Writing*, pp. 153-67. Edited by Joseph Pivato. Montreal: Guernica, 1985.

Caccia, Fulvio. *Sous le signe du Phénix.* Montreal: Guernica, 1985. 305pp.

Campanella, Mary, ed. *Proceedings of Symposium '77 on the Economic, Social, and Cultural Conditions of the Italian Canadian in the Hamilton-Wentworth Region.* Hamilton, Ontario: Italian-Canadian Federation of Hamilton, 1977. 72pp.

Campo, Alfredo. "Il congresso nazionale degli Italo-Canadese." *Il Veltro* 3-4, anno XXIX (May-August 1985): 515-18.

Canada. Department of Citizenship and Immigration. *Some Observations on Italian Immigrants in Toronto.* Ottawa: Economic and Social Research Division, Department of Citizenship and Immigration, 1961. 24pp.

Canada. Department of Manpower and Immigration. *Highlights from the Green Paper on Immigration and Population.* Canadian Immigration and Population Study. Ottawa: Information Canada,1975. 53pp. Bilingual.

Canada. Manpower and Immigration. *Immigration and Population Statistics.* Canadian Immigration and Population Study. Ottawa: Information Canada, 1974. 126pp.

Canada. Ministry of Health and Welfare. *The Agreement on Social Security between Italy and Canada.* Ottawa, 1979.

Canada. Multiculturalism Canada, Department of the Secretary of State of Canada. *Atlas of Residential Concentration for Census Metropolitan Area of Toronto.* Ottawa: Minister of Supply and Services, 1986. 127pp. Bilingual. One in a series of three atlases that also includes Montreal and Vancouver.

Canada. *Report of the Royal Commission on Bilingualism and Biculturalism.* Book IV: *The Contribution of the Other Ethnic Groups.* Ottawa: Information Canada, 1970; reprint ed., 1973. 352pp.

Canesi, Nanni. *La costituzione italiana e di altri 19 paesi di democrazia classica.* 2 vols. Rome: IPS, 1977. 1439pp.

Cappadocia, Ezio. "Becoming a Professor through the Early Post-war Years." Paper presented at the Third Annual

Elia Chair Lecture Series in Italian-Canadian Studies, York University, North York, Ontario, 26 February 1986. 61 leaves.

Carbone, Renzo. "Italians, Health and Italian-Canadians." Paper presented at the Third Annual Elia Chair Lecture Series in Italian-Canadian Studies, York University, North York, Ontario, 2 April 1986. 39 leaves.

Carr, Derek C. "Gli studi Italiani nell' università della Columbia Britannica." *Il Veltro* 1-2, anno XXIX (January-April 1985): 235-37.

Carraro, Joseph. "Unions and the Italian Community." *Polyphony* 7, no. 2 (Fall/Winter 1985): 105-06. Translation of article from *Canadian Mosaico*, February 1975.

Caussy, Devianee. *Residential Mobility of Italian Immigrants in Hamilton.* Ottawa: National Library of Canada. 1980. 122 leaves.

Chandler, S. Bernard. "Gli studi Italiani in Canada." *Il Veltro* 1-2, anno XXIX (January-April 1985): 219-26.

Ciavolella, Massimo. "La stampa Italiana in Canada." *Il Veltro* 3-4, anno XXIX (May-August 1985): 421-30.

Cipolla, Arnaldo. *Nell' America del Nord. Impressioni di un viaggio in Alaska, Stati Uniti e Canada.* Turin: Paravia, 1925. 344pp.

Clivio, Gianrenzo. "Italiese: A Language of Survival and Success in Toronto." Paper presented at the Second Annual Elia Lecture Series in Italian-Canadian Studies, York University, North York, Ontario, 26 February 1985. 16 leaves.

Clivio, Gianrenzo. "Italiese Glossary Report of Research." *University of Toronto Graduate* 5, no. 2 (Winter 1977): 1,7.

Clivio, Gianrenzo P. "Il punto sull' italiese." *Quaderni canadesi* 2, no. 3 (March-April 1978): 14.

Clivio, Gianrenzo P. "Su alcune caratteristiche dell' Italiese di Toronto." *Il Veltro* 3-4, anno XXIX (May-August 1985): 483-93.

Colalillo, Giuliana. "The Italian Immigrant Family." *Polyphony* 7, no. 2 (Fall/Winter 1985): 119-22.

Colalillo, Giuliana. "The Italian Immigrant Family: Continuity or Conflicts?" *Multiculturalism* 5, no. 3 (1982): 6-11.

Collenette, David. "Il contributo Italiano al multiculturalismo canadese." *Il Veltro* 1-2, anno XXIX (January-April 1985): 39-45.

Conte, Franco. *I lucani a Toronto.* Scarborough, Ontario: Litho Graphica, 1984. 182pp.

Conte, Franco. "Nuovo Mondo." *Polyphony* 4, no. 1 (Spring/Summer 1982): 126-27.

Cumbo, Enrico. "The Feast of the Madonna del Monte." *Polyphony* 5, no. 2 (Fall/Winter 1983): 84-85.

Cumbo, Enrico. "Material Culture and Ethnic Studies." *Polyphony* 9, no. 1 (Fall/Winter 1987): 79-82.

Cumbo, Enrico. "Recreational Activity at the Hamilton Venetian Club." *Polyphony* 7, no. 1 (Spring/Summer 1985): 59-63.

Cumbo, Enrico. "Sports and Inter-Ethnic Relations at Camp Petawawa." *Polyphony* 7, no. 1 (Spring/Summer 1985): 31-34.

Curtis, James E., and Lambert, Ronald D. "Opposition to Multiculturalism among Quebecois and English-Canadians." *Canadian Review of Sociology and Anthropology* 20, no. 2 (May 1983): 193-207.

D'Alfonso, Antonio. "The Road Between: Essentialism. For an Italian Culture in Quebec and Canada." In *Contrasts. Comparative Essays on Italian-Canadian Writing*, pp. 207-29. Edited by Joseph Pivato. Montreal: Guernica, 1985.

D'Ambrosio, Luigi, and D'Ambrosio, Elvira. *Cultural Retention of Italian-Canadian Youth: A Sociological Study*. Toronto: The Canadian Italian Business & Professional Association of Toronto, 1981. 81pp.

D'Andrea, Antonio. "Trent'anni in Canada. Frammenti di vita e di cultura." *Il Veltro* 1-2, anno XXIX (January-April 1985): 205-10.

Danesi, Marcel. "Canadian Italian: a Case in Point of How Language Adapts to Environment." *Polyphony* 7, no. 2 (Fall/Winter 1985): 111-14.

Danesi, Marcel. "Canadian Italian as a Marker of Ethnicity." *Nemla Italian Studies: Proceedings: Italian Section, Northeast Modern Language Association Conference* 7-8 (1983-84): 99-105.

Danesi, Marcel. "Ethnic 'Koines' and the Verbal Structuring of Reality: Psycholinguistic Observations on Canadian Italian." *Italian Canadiana* 3, no. 1 (Spring 1987): 113-23.

Danesi, Marcel. "L'insegnamento dell'Italiano ai discenti Italo-Canadesi." *Il Veltro* 3-4, anno XXIX (May-August 1985): 447-55.

Day, Robert D. "Ethnic Soccer Clubs in London, Canada: A Study in Assimilation." *International Review of Sport Sociology* 16, no. 1 (1981).

De Iuliis, Celestino. "Pier Giorgio di Cicco. A Poet Amongst Us." *Quaderni canadesi* 2, no. 3 (March-April 1978): 3-5.

De Rango, Rosanna. "My Elderly Sisters of Italy." *Canadian Woman Studies/les cahiers de la femme* 8, no. 2 (Summer 1987): 47-49.

Desaulniers, René. "Les Italiens au Canada." *Relations* 9, no. 100 (1949): 162-63.

De Stefanis Ciccone, Stefania. "Vancouver-Venezia: un singolare gemellaggio culturale." *Il Veltro* 3-4, anno XXIX (May-August 1985): 457-69.

Di Giovanni, Alberto. "L'insegnamento dell' italiano nell' 'Heritage Program'." *Il Veltro* 3-4, anno XXIX (May-August 1985): 439-45.

di Michele, Mary. "Writers from Invisible Cities." *Canadian Woman Studies/ les cahiers de la femme* 8, no. 2 (Summer 1987): 37-38.

Di Nardo, Jack. "Aging in the Italian Community." *Multiculturalism* 4, no. 1 (1980): 27-32.

Di Santo, Odoardo. "Forze Nuove." *Polyphony* 4, no. 1 (Spring/Summer 1982): 123-25.

Dobson, Lesley. "The Making of 'Franco'." *Multiculturalism* 1, no. 3 (1977): 26-28.

Doughty, Howard A. et al., eds. *Canadian Studies: Culture and Country*. Toronto: Wiley, 1976. Section on Italians, pp. 201-14.

Edwards, Caterina. "Italian-CanadianWriting: The Search for a Place and a Voice." Paper presented at the Third Annual Elia Chair Lecture Series in Italian-Canadian Studies,

York University, North York, Ontario, 19 March 1986. 36 leaves.

Erasmi, Gabriele. "La grammatica degli emigrati all'inizio del secolo precedente." *Italian Canadiana* 2, no. 1 (Spring 1986): 68-85.

FACI. *Brief to the Ontario Government Re Heritage Ontario. An Italian Association's View of Multiculturalism.* Toronto: FACI, [1970].

Forcese, Dennis. *The Canadian Class Structure*, 2nd ed. Toronto: McGraw-Hill Ryerson, 1980, pp. 43-52.

Framarin, Benito. *I Cattivi Pensieri di Don Smarto: Un prete Italiano in Canada.* Padua: Edizioni Messaggero, 1986. 350pp.

Franceschetti, Antonio. "La società canadese di Italianistica." *Il Veltro* 3-4, anno XXIX (May-August 1985): 525-31.

Fratta, Carla. "Traduzioni Italiane di testi letterari Quebecchesi." *Il Veltro* 3-4, anno XXIX (May-August 1985): 303-12.

Fulci, Francesco Paolo. "Le relazioni tra l'Italia e il Canada: realta e prospettive." *Il Veltro* 1-2, anno XXIX (January-April 1985): 21-31.

Gale, Donald T. "The Impact of Canadian Italians on Retail Functions and Facades in Vancouver, 1921-1961." In *Peoples of the Living Land: Geography of Cultural Diversity in B.C.*, pp. 107-24. Edited by Julian Vincent Minghi. Vancouver: Tantalis Research, 1972.

Garigue, Philippe. *The Association of Persons of Italian Descent in Montreal.* Montreal: Department of Sociology and Anthropology, McGill University, 1955. 100pp. Typescript.

Germano, Giovanni. *Gli italiani del canada occidentale: come nasce un centro comunitario* (The Italians of Western Canada: How a Community Centre Is Born). Florence: Giunti Marzocco, 1977. Text with English translation. 192pp.

Giulano, Bruce B. *Sacro o Profano? A Consideration of Four Italian-Canadian Religious Festivals.* Canadian Centre for Folk Culture Studies, Mercury Series Paper no. 17. Ottawa: National Museums of Man, 1976. 64pp.

Goggio, Emilio. "The Italian Contribution to the Development of Music in Ontario." *Canadian Review of Music and Art* 4, nos. 3-4 (1944): 29-32. Also Vol. 4, nos. 5-6 (1945-46).

Goggio, Emilio. "Italian Influences in the Cultural Life of Old Montreal." *Canadian Modern Languages Review* 9, no. 1 (1952).

Gold, Gerald. "Italians and French: Two Ways of Being Different in Northern Ontario." Paper presented at the Second Annual Elia Lecture Series in Italian-Canadian Studies, York University, North York, Ontario, 7 March 1985. 61 leaves.

Greenwood, M. *Some Observations on Italian Immigrants in Toronto.* Ottawa: Department of Citizenship and Immigration. n.d.

Grohovaz, Gianni A. *E con rispetto parlando e al microfono, Gianni Grohovaz.* Toronto: Casa Editrice Sono Me, 1983. 25pp.

Grohovaz, Gianni A. "If You Don't Know How to Play Bocce, Don't Come a Courting My Sister." *Polyphony* 7, no. 1 (Spring/Summer 1985): 129-30.

Grohovaz, Gianni A. *Per Ricordar le Cose che Ricordo.* Toronto: Dufferin Press, 1974.

Grohovaz, Gianni A. "A Quest for Heritage: Piccolo Teatro Italiano." *Polyphony* 5, no. 2 (Fall-Winter 1983): 47-55.

Grohovaz, Gianni A. "See You at Brandon Hall. Oh! ... I Mean the Italo-Canadian Recreation Club." *Polyphony* 7, no. 2 (Fall/Winter 1985): 98-103.

Grohovaz, Gianni A. "Toronto's Italian Press after the Second World War." *Polyphony* 4, no. 1 (Spring/Summer 1982): 105-13.

Harney, Robert F. "Homo Ludens and Ethnicity." *Polyphony* 7, no. 1 (Spring/Summer 1985): 1-12.

Hartley, Norman. "Toronto Italian: New World Language." In *The Toronto Book: An Anthology of Writings Past and Present*, pp. 132-34. Edited by William Kilbourn. Toronto: Macmillan, 1976.

Helling, R.A. "The Position of Negroes, Chinese and Italians in the Social Structure of Windsor, Ontario." A report submitted to the Ontario Human Rights Commission, December 1965. Windsor, Department of Sociology and Anthropology, University of Windsor, 1965. 124pp.

Iacovetta, Franca. "Trying to Make Ends Meet: An Historical Look at Italian Immigrant Women, the State and Family Survival Strategies in Post-War Toronto." *Canadian Woman Studies/les cahiers de la femme* 8, no. 2 (Summer 1987): 6-11.

Ianni, Ronald. "Italian-Canadians in the Legal Profession: A Presence Without a Precedent." Paper presented at the Third Annual Murray A. Elia lecture series in Italian-Canadian Studies, York University, North York, Ontario, 5 February 1986. 45 leaves.

Iannucci, Susan. La poesia Italo-Canadese." *Il Veltro* 3-4, anno XXIX (May-August 1985): 347-65.

Jansen, Clifford J. "Le comunitâ Italiane nella Columbia Britannica." *Il Veltro* 1-2, anno XXIX (January-April 1985): 191-96.

Jansen, Clifford J. "Community Organization of Italians in Toronto." In *The Canadian Ethnic Mosaic*, pp. 310-26. Edited by Leo Driedger. Toronto: McClelland & Stewart, 1978.

Jansen, Clifford J. *Fact-book on Italians in Canada*. North York, Ontario: Institute for Social Research, York University, 1981. 96pp. (First edition with Lee R. LaCavera, 1981. 84pp.)

Jansen, Clifford J. "Inter-Ethnic Marriages." *International Journal of Comparative Sociology* 13, nos. 3-4 (1982).

Jansen, Clifford J. "The Italian Community in Toronto." In *Minority Canadians*. Vol. 2: *Immigrant Groups*, pp. 207-15. Edited by Jean Leonard Elliott. Scarborough, Ontario: Prentice-Hall, 1971.

Jansen, Clifford J. *The Italians of Vancouver: A Case Study of Internal Differentiation of an Ethnic Group*. North York, Ontario: Institute for Behavioural Research, York University, 1981. 114 leaves.

Jansen, Clifford J. "Leadership in the Italian Ethnic Group in Toronto." *International Migration Review* 4, no. 1 (1969): 25-43.

Jansen, Clifford J., and Gallucci, John F. *A Study of Multiculturalism and Italian Media.* Toronto: Wintario Citizenship and Multicultural Program, 1977. 63pp.

Jansen, Clifford J., and Paasche, Gottfried. "Unity and Disunity in Two Ethnic Groups in Toronto." In *The Underside of Toronto*, pp. 182-96. Edited by W.E. Mann. Toronto: McClelland & Stewart, 1970.

Kalbach, Warren E. *The Effect of Immigration on Population.* Canadian Immigration and Population Study. Ottawa: Information Canada, 1974. 93pp.

Kalbach, Warren E. "Growth and Distribution of Canada's Ethnic Populations, 1871-1971." In *The Canadian Ethnic Mosaic: A Quest for Identity.* Canadian Ethnic Studies Association Series Vol. 6, pp. 82-104. Edited by Leo Driedger. Toronto: McClelland & Stewart, 1978; reprint ed., 1979.

Kalbach, Warren E., and McVey, Wayne W. *The Demographic Bases of Canadian Society.* Toronto: McGraw-Hill Ryerson, 1971; 2nd ed., 1979, pp. 39-66, 176-219.

Kallman, Helmut, ed. *Catalogue of Canadian Composers.* Rev. ed. Ottawa: CBC, 1952, p. 31. On Lucio Agostini.

Keeble, K. Corey. "L'arte Italiana a Toronto." *Il Veltro* 3-4, anno XXIX (May-August 1985): 373-84.

King, Lorraine. "Customs of Italian Immigrants." *Canadian Nurse Journal* 60 (1964).

Kuitunen, Maddalena. "La formazione del docente d'Italiano in Ontario." *Il Veltro* 3-4, anno XXIX (May-August 1985): 432-38.

Lanphier, Michael C. "Ethnicity and Occupation Prestige Ranking: Socio-Demographic and Regional Perspectives." North York, Ontario: Institute for Behavioural Research, York University, 1981.

Leone, Laureano. "National Congress of Italian Canadians Report." In *Briefs on Multiculturalism*. Ottawa: Minister of State - Multiculturalism, 1978, pp. 58-67.

Lombardi, Johnny. "A Humane Look at the Unity Question." In *The Canadian Alternative*, pp. 50-54. Edited by Hédi Bouraoui. Downsview, Ontario: ECW Press, 1979.

McKay, J. "Entity vs. Process Approaches to Ethnic Relations and Ethnic Identity: A Case Study of Ethnic Soccer Clubs in Toronto's Italian Community." *Canadian Ethnic Studies* 12, no. 3 (1980): 56-80.

Marchetto, Ezio. "The Catholic Church and Italian Immigration to Toronto: an Overview." *Polyphony* 7, no. 2 (Fall/Winter 1985): 106-10.

Martucci, Jean. "Il Quebec e l'Italia." *Il Veltro* 1-2, anno XXIX (January-April 1985): 181-89.

Mastrangelo, Rocco. *The Italian Canadians*. Scarborough, Ontario: Van Nostrand Reinhold, 1979. 64pp.

Menchini, Camillo. *Chiesa della Madonna della Difesa: Guida Storico Descrittiva*. Montreal: Paroisse N.D. de la Defense, 1965. 71pp.

Metro Toronto Italo-Canadian Commercial Directory. Toronto: Charles L. Caccia & Associates, 1962-71.

Minni, C.D. "The Short Story as an Ethnic Genre." In *Contrasts. Comparative Essays on Italian-Canadian Writing*, pp. 61-76. Edited by Joseph Pivato. Montreal: Guernica, 1985.

Molinaro, Julius A. "Italian Outside the Classroom at the University of Toronto (1881-1940)." *Italian Canadiana* 2, no. 1 (Spring 1986): 14-30.

Molinaro, Matie Armstrong. "The Randel 'Venus': A Lost Correggio." *Italian Canadiana* 3, no. 1 (Spring 1987): 124-48.

Montero, Gloria. *The Immigrants*. Toronto: James Lorimer, 1977, pp. 57-61, 77-78, 85-88, 150-54, 160, 165, 185, 218-19.

Murta, Jack Burnett. "Il contributo Italiano al multiculturalismo canadese." *Il Veltro* 1-2, anno XXIX (January-April 1985): 11-19.

Nagata, Judith A. "One Vine, Many Branches: Internal Differentiation in Canadian Ethnic Groups." In *Two Nations, Many Cultures: Ethnic Groups in Canada*, pp. 173-81. Edited by Jean Leonard Elliott. Scarborough, Ontario: Prentice-Hall, 1979.

Napolitano. *Troppo grano sotto la neve. Un inverno al Canadà, con una visita a Ford*. Milan: Ceschina, 1936. 490pp.

Ng, Roxana, and Ramirez, Judith. *Immigrant Housewives in Canada: A Report*. Toronto: Immigrant Women's Centre, 1981. 76pp.

O'Bryan, K.G., Reitz, J.G., and Kuplowska, O.M. *Non-Official Languages*. Ottawa: Ministry of Supply and Services, 1976.

Ontario. Ministry of Citizenship and Culture. *A Study of Multiculturalism & Italian Media*. Toronto: Wintario Citizenship & Multiculturalism Program, 1977. 63 leaves.

Order of the Sons of Italy of Ontario. *Submission to the Special Joint Committee of the Senate and the House of Commons on Immigration.* Ottawa, 1967, pp. 728-30.

Osborne, John. "La storia dell'arte Italiana in Canada." *Il Veltro* 3-4, anno XXIX (May-August 1985): 367-71.

Paci, F.G. "Tasks of the Canadian Novelist Writing on Immigrant Themes." In *Contrasts. Comparative Essays on Italian-Canadian Writing*, pp. 35-60. Edited by Joseph Pivato. Montreal: Guernica, 1985.

Paldi, Julio. *Report on the Italians in Metro Toronto.* Toronto: Citizenship Board of the Ontario Provincial Secretary, 1970. 83pp.

Pasquarelli, Mirella. "Lexical Interference in Depth: The Technical Vocabulary of Italian-Canadian Carpenters." Paper presented at the Elia Chair Seminar Series in Italian-Canadian Studies, York University, North York, Ontario, 26 February 1986. 34 leaves.

Pasquarelli, Mirella. "La società Canadese di linguistica e didattica Italiana." *Il Veltro* 3-4, anno XXIX (May-August 1985): 533-37.

Pedrone, John. *A Short History of the Italian People in Canada.* Toronto: Italian Immigrant Aid Society, 1958.

Perin, Roberto. "Il convegno internazionale, 'L'esperienza degli immigrati italiani in Canada' (Roma, 9-13 maggio 1984)." *Studi Emigrazione/Etudes Migrations* no. 77 (March 1985): 141-44.

Perry, Harriett. "The Metonymic Definition of the Female and the Concept of Honour Among Italian Immigrant Families in Toronto." In *The Italian Immigrant Woman in North America*, pp. 222-31. Edited by Betty Boyd Caroli, Robert F. Harney, and Lydio Tomasi. Toronto: MHSO, 1978.

Picchione, John. "I giovani italo-canadesi: considerazione socio-culturale." In *I giovani italo-canadese, i loro problemi, le loro aspirazioni*. Rome: Edizione FILEF, 1984.

Picone, Michelangelo. "Dante in Canada." *Il Veltro* 1-2, anno XXIX (January-April, 1985): 247-56.

Pietropaolo, Domenico. "Aspects of English Interference on the Italian Language in Toronto." *Canadian Modern Language Review* 30, no. 3 (March 1974): 234-41.

Pineo, Peter C. "The Extended Family in a Working Class Area of Hamilton." In *Canadian Society: Sociological Perspectives*, pp. 115-25. Edited by Bernard R. Blishen et al. Toronto: MacMillan, 3rd abridged ed., 1971. First published 1968.

Pivato, Joseph. "Ethnic Writing and Comparative Canadian Literature." In *Contrasts: Comparative Essays on Italian-Canadian Writing*, pp. 15-34. Edited by Joseph Pivato. Montreal:Guernica, 1985.

Pivato, Joseph. "Italian Writers in Ontario: a Brief Overview." *Polyphony* 7, no. 2 (Fall/Winter 1985): 133-36.

Pivato, Joseph. "A Literature of Exile: Italian Language Writing in Canada." In *Contrasts: Comparative Essays on Italian-Canadian Writing*, pp. 169-88. Edited by Joseph Pivato. Montreal: Guernica, 1985.

Politi, Vittorio. "Gli istituti Italiani di cultura in Canada." *Il Veltro* 3-4, anno XXIX (May-August 1985): 503-14.

Porter, John. *The Vertical Mosaic: An Analysis of Social Class and Power in Canada*. Toronto: University of Toronto Press, 1965; reprint ed., 1972. Chap. 3.

Potvin, Gilles. "La musica Italiana in Canada." *Il Veltro* 3-4, anno XXIX (May-August 1985): 397-402.

Pratley, Gerald. "La presenza del cinema Italiano in Canada." *Il Veltro* 3-4, anno XXIX (May-August 1985): 415-20.

Predelli, Maria Bendinelli. "L'associazione dei professori d'Italiano del Quebec." *Il Veltro* 3-4, anno XXIX (May-August 1985): 519-24.

Pucci, Antonio. "Ethnicity Is Canadian." *Northern Mosaic* 1, no. 2 (December 1975).

Ramirez, Bruno. "Immigration et rapports familiaux chez les Italiens du Québec." *Quaderni Culturali* 2, no. 1 (1982): 17-23. (Similar version in *Critère* 33 [Spring 1982].)

Reitz, Jeffrey G. "Language and Ethnic Community Survival." In *Ethnicity and Ethnic Relations in Canada*, pp. 111-29. Edited by Jay E. Goldstein and Rita M. Bienvenue. Toronto: Butterworth and Co., 1980.

"The Return Journey in Italian Canadian Literature." *Canadian Literature* 106 (Fall 1985): 169-76.

Ricci, Giuseppe. *L'Orfano di Padre. Le Memorie di Giuseppe Ricci*. Toronto: Astra, 1981. 253pp.

Richert, Jean Pierre. "The Impact of Ethnicity on the Perception of Heroes and Historical Symbols." *Canadian Review of Sociology and Anthropology* 11, no. 2 (May 1974): 156-73.

Rossi, Erno Delano, and Iaconis, Giuseppe. "The Italians." In *Many Cultures, Many Heritages*, pp. 238-87. Edited by Norman Sheffe. Toronto: McGraw-Hill Ryerson, 1975. Available in French.

Ryder, N.B. "The Interpretation of Origin Statistics." *Canadian Journal of Economics and Political Science* 24, no. 4 (November 1955): 466-79.

Salvatore, Filippo. "The Italian Writers of Quebec: Language, Culture and Politics." In *Contrasts: Comparative Essays on Italian-Canadian Writing*, pp. 189-206. Edited by Joseph Pivato. Montreal: Guernica, 1985.

Sciff-Zamaro, Roberta. "Black Madonna: A Search for the Great Mother." In *Contrasts. Comparative Essays on Italian-Canadian Writing*, pp. 77-99. Edited by Joseph Pivato. Montreal: Guernica, 1985.

Sharma, R.D. "Trends in Demographic and Socio-Economic Characteristics of the Metropolitan Toronto Population." North York, Ontario: Institute for Behavioural Research, York University, 1981.

Spelt, Jacob. *Toronto*. Canadian Cities Series. Toronto: Collier Macmillan, 1973, pp. 104-09.

Squilla, Gaetano. *I miei tre viaggi nel Canadà e negli Stati Uniti*. Frosinone: Tipografia dell' Abbazia di Casamari, 1969.

Stewart, Pamela D. "Gli studi Italiani nel Quebec." *Il Veltro* 1-2, anno XXIX (January-April 1985): 227-33.

Sturino, Franc. "Family and Kin Cohesion Among Southern Italian Immigrants in Toronto." In *Canadian Families: Ethnic Variations*, pp. 84-104. Edited by K. Ishwaran. Toronto: McGraw-Hill Ryerson, 1980. (Earlier version in *The Italian Immigrant Woman in North America*. Edited by Betty Boyd Caroli, Robert F. Harney, and Lydio Tomasi. Toronto: MHSO, 1978.)

Sturino, Franc. "The Social Mobility of Italian Canadians: 'Outside' and 'Inside' Concepts of Mobility." *Polyphony* 7, no. 2 (Fall/Winter 1985): 123-27.

Stymeist, David H. "Non-Native Ethnicity in Crow Lake." In *Ethnicity and Ethnic Relations in Canada*, pp. 27-45. Edited by Jay E. Goldstein and Rita M. Bienvenue. Toronto: Butterworth and Co., 1980.

Taschereau, Sylvie. "Un ministère en quête d'identité." *Quaderni Culturali* 2, no. 1 (1982): 1-4.

Temelini, Walter. "The Growth of Sports Involvement in the Windsor Area." *Polyphony* 7, no. 1 (Spring/Winter 1985): 21-26.

Tomasi, Lydio. "The Italian Community in Toronto: A Demographic Profile." *International Migration Review* 11, no. 4 (Winter 1977): 486-513.

Trovato, Frank. "Canadian Ethnic Fertility." *Sociological Focus* 14, no. 1 (1981).

Trovato, Frank, and Burch, T.K. "Minority Group Status and Fertility in Canada." *Canadian Ethnic Studies* 12, no. 3 (1980).

Velikonja, Joseph. "Gli italiani nelle città canadesi. Appunti geografici." *Estratto di Atti del XIX Congresso Geografico Italiano 1964*. Como, 1965, pp. 371-88.

Viaggio del presidente Gronchi negli Stati Uniti e Canadà (27 febbraio/14 marzo 1956). Milan: Alfieri and Lacroix, 1956.

Wolfgang, Aaron. "The Teacher and Non-Verbal Behaviour in the Multicultural Classroom." In *Nonverbal Behaviour: Applications and Cultural Implications*. Edited by Aaron Wolfgang. Toronto: Ontario Institute for Studies in Education, 1979.

Yeo, W.B. "Canada's Curious Usage of Italian Place Names (1850's-1910)." *Canadian Geographer* 98, no. 1 (1979): 58-61.

Ziegler, Suzanne. *Characteristics of Italian Householders in Metropolitan Toronto.* North York, Ontario: York Survey Research Centre (Institute for Behavioural Research), York University, 1972. 122 leaves.

Zucchi, John E. "Società Italiana di Copper Cliff." *Polyphony* 2, no. 1 (Winter 1979): 29-30.

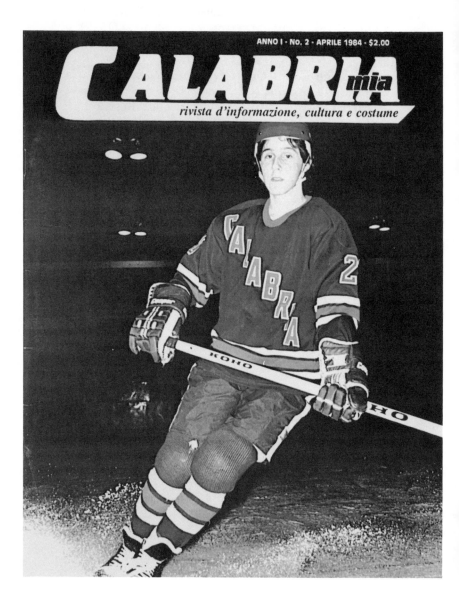

ANNO I · No. 2 · APRILE 1984 · $2.00

CALABRIA mia

rivista d'informazione, cultura e costume

SECTION 3: EDUCATION AND SOCIALIZATION

Allevato, Costanza. "The Status of Italian Immigrant Women in Canada." *Canadian Woman Studies/les cahiers de la femme* 8, no. 2 (Summer 1987): 12-13.

Allodi, F.A. "Accident Neurosis; Whatever Happened to Male Hysteria?" *Canadian Psychiatric Association Journal* 19, no. 3 (1974): 291-96.

Allodi, F.A. "Help-Seeking Patterns of the Italians in Toronto." *Canadian Journal of Public Health* 58, no. 10 (October 1967): 441-43.

Allodi, F.A. "The Italians in Toronto: Mental Health Problems of an Immigrant Community." In *Social Deviance in Canada*, pp. 251-63. Edited by W.E. Mann. Toronto: Copp Clark, 1971.

Anisef, Paul. "Consequences of Ethnicity for Educational Plans among Grade 12 Students." In *Education of Immigrant Students. Issues and Answers.* Symposium Series no. 5, pp. 122-36. Edited by Aaron Wolfgang. Toronto: Ontario Institute for Studies in Education, 1975.

Balakrishnan, T.R. "Changing Patterns of Ethnic Residential Segregation in the Metropolitan Areas of Canada." *Canadian Review of Sociology and Anthropology* 19 (1982): 92-110.

Bancroft, George W. *Outreach for Understanding: A Report of the Intercultural Seminar Program Conducted in Toronto between 1973 and 1975*. Toronto: Ministry of Culture and Recreation, 1977, pp. 81-90.

Battistelli, Fabrizio. "L'Autonomia culturale come strumento di assimilaizone: i mass media italiani nella comunità immigrata di Toronto." *Rassegna Italiana di Sociologia* 16, no. 3 (1975): 449-65.

Berry, John W., Kalin, Rudolf, and Taylor, Donald M. "Multiculturalism and Ethnic Attitudes in Canada." In *Ethnicity and Ethnic Relations in Canada*, pp. 259-78. Edited by Jay E. Goldstein and Rita M. Bienvenue. Toronto: Butterworth, 1980.

Breda, Nadia et al. *Approach the Italian Poor*. Toronto: Italian Immigrant Aid Society, 1971.

Breton, Raymond. *The Ethnic Community as a Resource in Relation to Group Problems: Perceptions and Attitudes*. Toronto: Centre for Urban and Community Studies, University of Toronto, 1981.

Cappon, Paul. *Conflits entre Néo-Canadiens et Francophones de Montréal*. Québec: Les Presses de l'Université Laval, 1974. Chap. 3: Comparaison entre les attitudes collectives et le comportement des groupes allemands, italiens et grecs, pp. 99-101.

Chee, Alice et al. *Italians in Canada*. Scarborough, Ontario: Scarborough Board of Education, 1976. 66pp.

Colalillo, Giuliana. "Patterns of Socialization among Italian Adolescent Girls." *Journal of Baltic Studies* 10, no. 1 (1979): 43-50.

Corrigan, B. "Modern Italian Studies." *University of Toronto Quarterly* 32 (January 1963): 193-98.

Corsini, M.V. "The Student of Italian - Who is he?" *Canadian Modern Language Review* 31 (1975): 424-27.

Costa, Elio, and di Santo, Odoardo. "The Italian-Canadian Child, His Family, and the Canadian School System." In *Must Schools Fail?* pp. 242-50. Edited by Niall Byrne and Jack Quarter. Toronto: McClelland & Stewart, 1972.

COSTI. *The Report on the COSTI Two-Way Value Translation Program, October 1976. A report on a project to alleviate teacher-parent-student (Italian) problems in four Metro schools.* Toronto: COSTI, 1976.

D'Antini, Bert. *Papers on the Italian Community: The Quiet Desperation of the Immigrant.* Ontario Ministry of Culture and Recreation, Multicultural Development Branch, 1976. 7 leaves. Mimeographed.

Danesi, Marcel. "Ethnic Languages and Acculturation: the Case of Italo-Canadians." *Canadian Ethnic Studies* 17, no. 1 (Summer 1985): 98-103.

Danziger, Kurt. "The Acculturation of Italian Immigrant Girls." In *The Canadian Family.* Rev. ed., pp. 200-12. Edited by K. Ishwaren. Toronto: Holt, Rinehart and Winston of Canada, 1976. (Earlier version in *Sociology Canada: Readings.* Edited by C. Beattie and S. Cripdole. Toronto: Butterworth, 1974.)

Danziger, Kurt. "The Acculturation of Italian Immigrant Girls in Canada." *International Journal of Psychology* 9, no. 2 (1974): 129-37.

Danziger, Kurt. "Attitudes to parental control and adolescents' aspirations: A comparison of immigrants and non-immigrants." In *Childhood and Adolescence in Canada*, pp. 179-94. Edited by K. Ishwaren. Toronto: McGraw-Hill Ryerson, [1979].

Danziger, Kurt. "Differences in Acculturation and Patterns of Socialization among Italian Immigrant Families." In

Socialization and Values in Canadian Society. Vol. 2: *Socialization, Social Stratification and Ethnicity*, pp. 129-57. Edited by Robert M. Pike and Elia Zureik. Toronto: McClelland & Stewart, 1975.

Danziger, Kurt. "The Socialization of Immigrant Children." North York, Ontario: Institute for Behavioural Research, York University, 1971. 171 leaves.

Danziger, Kurt. *Sources of Instability in the Distribution of Control among Italian Immigrant and Non-Immigrant Families in Canada*. North York, Ontario: York University, Department of Psychology Reports, no. 56, 1977. 11 leaves.

Darroch, A. Gordon. "Another Look at Ethnicity Stratification and Social Mobility in Canada." *Canadian Journal of Sociology* 4, no. 1 (Winter, 1979): 1-25. Reprinted in *Ethnicity and Ethnic Relations in Canada*, pp. 203-29. Edited by Jay E. Goldstein and Rita M. Bienvenue. Toronto: Butterworth, 1980.

Darroch, A. Gordon, and Marston, W.G. "The Social Class Basis of Ethnic Residential Segregation: the Canadian Case." *American Journal of Sociology* (1977).

Delfino, Angelo. "Italian Immigrant Aid Society: an Historical Outline." *Polyphony* 7, no. 2 (Fall/Winter 1985): 115-18.

Denis, Ann B. "The Relationship between Ethnicity and Educational Aspirations of Post-Secondary Students in Toronto and Montreal." In *Ethnic Canadians*. Edited by M.L. Kovacks. Regina: Ministry of Culture and Education, 1978.

Draft Report of the Work Group on Multicultural Programs. Toronto: Board of Education for the City of Toronto, 20 May 1975. 223 leaves.

Dreidger, Leo, and Mezoff, Richard A. "Ethnic Prejudice and Discrimination in Winnipeg High Schools." *Canadian Journal of Sociology* 6, no. 1 (1981).

Ferguson, Edith. *Immigrant Integration: Our Obligations – Political, Social and Economic – to the 1,700,000 People Who Have Come to Ontario in the Past Quarter Century: a Report*. Toronto: Ontario Economic Council, [1970]. 55pp.

Ferguson, Edith. *Immigrants and Education. A Talk Given at a Conference on Immigration at Centennial College, Scarborough, 1 May 1975*. Toronto: Ministry of Culture and Recreation. 10pp.

Ferguson, Edith. *Immigrants in Canada*. Toronto: University of Toronto Press, 1977.

Ferguson, Edith. *Newcomers in Transition: An Experimental Study Project conducted by the International Institute of Metropolitan Toronto to Study the Relations Between Rural Immigrants and Toronto's Community Services*. Toronto, 1964. 128pp.

Filef. "Il dramma dell' identità dei giovani italo-quebechesi." *Emigrazione* 12 (1981).

Gillies, Alba, and Polsinelli, Angela. "Using Television to Reach Non-English Speaking Immigrants." *Tesl Talk* [Teaching English as a Second Language] 13, no. 3 (Summer 1982): 82-86.

Goldlust, John, and Richmond, Anthony H. "Factors Associated with Commitment to and Identification with Canada." In *Identities: The Impact of Ethnicity on Canadian Society*. Canadian Ethnic Studies Association Series Vol. 5, pp. 132-53. Edited by Wsevolod Isajiw. Toronto: Peter Martin, 1977.

Grande, Anthony. "A Transition Program for Young Immigrant Children." In *Education of Immigrant Students: Issues and Answers*. Symposium Series no. 5, pp. 35-45. Edited by Aaron Wolfgang. Toronto: Ontario Institute for Studies in Education, 1975.

Grande, Gregory. "COSTI: I.I.A.S.: Social Services in the Italian Community (1952-1985)." *Italian Canadiana* 3, no. 1 (Spring 1987): 92-112.

Greenglass, Esther R. "A Comparison of Maternal Communication Style between Immigrant Italian and Second-Generation Italian Women Living in Canada." *Journal of Cross-Cultural Psychology* 3, no. 2 (1972): 185-92. (Also in *Social Psychology: The Canadian Context*, pp. 335-44. Edited by J.W. Berry and G.J.S. Wilde. Toronto: McClelland & Stewart, 1972.)

Greenglass, Esther R. "Italian Mothers in Canada." *Journal of Ontario Association of Children's Aid Societies* 14, no. 10 (December 1971): 1-5.

Grygier, Tadeusz. "Integration of Four Ethnic Groups in Canadian Society: English, German, Hungarian, Italian." In *Sounds Canadian: Languages and Cultures in Multi-Ethnic Society*. Canadian Ethnic Studies Association Series Vol. 4, pp. 158-86. Edited by Paul M. Migus. Toronto: Peter Martin, 1975.

Grygier, Tadeusz. "The Bottom of a Tilted Mosaic: The Italian Community in Urban Canada." *Education, Change and Society: A Sociology of Canadian Education*, pp. 204-10. Edited by Richard A. Carlton et al. Toronto: Gage, 1977.

Hobart, Charles W. *Italian Immigrants in Edmonton: Adjustment and Integration*. Research Report of Royal Commission on Bilingualism and Biculturalism no. 8. 2 vols. Ottawa, 1967. 654pp.

Hull, I.L. "Special Problems of Italian Families." *Proceeding of the National Conference of Social Workers*. 1924, pp. 288-91.

Isajiw, Wsevolod W. *Ethnic Identity Retention*. Toronto: Centre for Urban and Community Studies, University of Toronto, 1981.

Isajiw, Wsevolod W., and Makabe, Tomoke. *Socialization as a Factor in Ethnic Identity Retention*. Toronto: Centre for Urban and Community Studies, University of Toronto, 1982.

Jansen, Clifford J. "Assimilation in Theory and Practice: A Case Study of Italians in Toronto." In *Social Process and Institution: The Canadian Case*, pp. 466-74. Edited by J.E. Gallagher & R.D. Lambert. Toronto: Holt, Rinehart & Winston of Canada Ltd., 1971.

Jansen, Clifford J. *Education and Social Mobility of Immigrants: A Pilot Study Focusing on Italians in Vancouver*. North York, Ontario: Institute for Behavioural Research, York University, 1981. 100 leaves.

Jansen, Clifford J. "Istruzione e multiculturalismo." In *I giovani italo-canadesi, i loro problemi, le loro aspirazioni*. Rome: Edizione FILEF, 1984.

Jansen, Clifford. "Italian Children and the Education System." Paper presented at the First Annual Elia Chair Lecture Series in Italian-Canadian Studies, York University, North York, Ontario, 1 March 1984. 44 leaves.

Jansen, Clifford J. "Italians in the Multicultural Society of the Eighties." *Polyphony* 7, no. 2 (Fall/Winter 1985): 128-31.

Jansen, Clifford. "Social and Economic Improvement of Italian-Canadians, 1971-1981." Paper presented at the

Third Annual Elia Lecture Series in Italian-Canadian
Studies, York University, North York, Ontario, 5 March
1986. 36 leaves.

Kalbach, Warren E. *Ethnic Residential Segregation and its
Significance for the Individual in an Urban Setting.*
Toronto: Centre for Urban and Community Studies,
University of Toronto, 1981.

Lawton, S.B., and O'Neill, S.P. "Ethnic Segregation in
Toronto's Elementary Schools." *Alberta Journal of
Educational Research* 19, no. 39 (1973): 195-201.

Lind, Loren. "New Canadianism: Melting the Ethnics in
Toronto Schools." In *The Politics of the Canadian Public
School*, pp. 103-17. Edited by George Martell. Toronto:
James Lewis & Samuel, 1974.

Loconte, Angela. *A Comparison of Behaviour and Attitudes of
Italian and Non-Italian Adolescent Canadian Females.*
Ottawa: National Library of Canada, 1982. 2 microfiche,
166 frames.

McDiarmid, Garnet. "Curriculum Development Is People
Development." In *Education of Immigrant Students:
Issues and Answers.* Symposium Series no. 5, pp. 184-91.
Edited by Aaron Wolfgang. Toronto: Ontario Institute for
Studies in Education, 1975.

McQuillan, Barry. "A Cross-Section of Cultures: Education
Week at Harbourfront." *Multiculturalism* 1, no. 2 (1977):
13-15.

Malzberg, Benjamin. *Mental Disease in Canada 1950-1952
Among Italian-Born.* Albany, New York: Research
Foundation for Mental Hygiene, 1963. 41pp.

Mann, W.E., and Hanley, L.G. "The Mafia in Canada." In *Deviant Behaviour in Canada.* Edited by W.E. Mann. n.p.: Social Science Publication, 1968.

Masemann, Vandra. "Immigrant Students' Perceptions of Occupational Programs." In *Education of Immigrant Students: Issues and Answers* Symposium Series no. 5, pp. 107-21. Edited by Aaron Wolfgang. Toronto: Ontario Institute for Studies in Education, 1975.

Maykovich, Minako K. "A Comparative Study of Japanese, Italian and Mennonite Canadians: Aspirations Versus Achievements." *International Review of Sociology* 1, no. 1 (March 1971): 13-26.

Maykovich, Minako K. "Ethnic Variation in Success Value." In *Socialization and Values in Canadian Society.* Vol. 2: *Socialization, Social Stratification and Ethnicity,* pp. 158-79. Edited by Robert M. Pike and Elia Zureik. Toronto: McClelland & Stewart, 1975.

Menniti, P. "Scenes of Two Cultures – The Need for Italian-Canadian Textbooks." *Canadian Journal of Italian Studies* 4, nos. 1-2 (1981): 175-78.

Mollica, Anthony. "Italians in Ontario." *Canadian Modern Language Review* 22, no. 3 (1966): 19-23.

Mosher, Loren R. "Radical Deinstitutionalization: The Italian Experience." *International Journal of Mental Health* 11, no. 4 (Winter 1982-83): 129-36.

Nagata, Judith A., Rayfield, Joan, and Ferraris, Mary. *English Language Classes for Immigrant Women with Pre-School Children.* North York, Ontario: Institute for Behavioural Research, York University, 1970. 116 leaves.

North York Board of Education. *Our Italian Population in North York*. North York, Ontario: Board of Education for the Borough of North York, 1972.

Palmer, Robin. "Processes of Estrangement and Disengagement in an Italian Emigrant Community." *New Community* 8, no. 3 (Winter 1980): 277-87.

Parai, Louis. *Immigration and Emigration of Professional and Skilled Manpower during the Post-War Period*. Special Study no. 1, Economic Council of Canada. Ottawa: The Queen's Printer, 1965. 249pp.

Parthun, M.L. "Incidence of Mental Illness among Italians in an English-Canadian City." *International Migration Review* 8, no. 3 (Fall 1974): 474ff.

Perillo, Carmen. "Multicultural Policy: Women Beware." *Canadian Woman Studies/les cahiers de la femme* 8, no. 2 (Summer 1987): 27-29.

Phelan, Josephine. "A Programme for the Italian Community." *Ontario Library Review* 47 (November 1963): 168-70.

Pichini, Lia. "Two Generations in Conflict: Sex Role Expectations Among Italian-Canadian Women." *Canadian Woman Studies/les cahiers de la femme* 8, no. 2 (Summer 1987): 22-23.

Pineo, Peter C. "The Social Standing of Ethnic and Racial Groupings." In *Ethnicity and Ethnic Relations in Canada*, pp. 185-201. Edited by Jay E. Goldstein and Rita M. Bienvenue. Toronto: Butterworth, 1980. (Also appeared in *Canadian Review of Sociology and Anthropology* 14, no. 2 [May 1977], pp. 147-57.)

Pisa Profili, Claudia. "La comunità italiana in Canada: alcuni dati e considerazioni. I problemi delle donne italo-canadese nel mondo di lavoro." In *I giovani italo-canadese, i loro problemi, i loro aspirazioni.* Rome: Edizione FILEF, 1984.

Porter, John. *Canadian Social Structure: A Statistical Profile,* pp. 75-85. Toronto: McClelland & Stewart, 1967; reprint ed. 1969.

Purbhoo, Mary, and Shapson, Stanley M. *Transition From Italian: The First Year.* Toronto: Research Department, Board of Education for the City of Toronto, September 1975. 99pp.

Ramcharan, Subhas. "Special Problems of Immigrant Children in the Toronto School System." In *Education of Immigrant Students: Issues and Answers.* Symposium Series no. 5, pp. 95-106. Edited by Aaron Wolfgang. Toronto: Ontario Institute for Studies in Education, 1975.

Rayfield, J.R. "Maria in Markham Street: Italian Immigrants and Language-Learning in Toronto." *Ethnic Groups* 1, no. 2 (1976): 133-50.

Rees-Powell, A. "Differentials in the Integration of Dutch and Italian Immigrants in Edmonton." *International Migration* 4, no. 3 (1966): 100-13.

Reitz, Jeffrey C. *The Survival of Ethnic Groups.* Toronto: McGraw-Hill Ryerson, 1980.

Reitz, Jeffrey C., Calzavara, Liviana, and Dasko, Donna. *Ethnic Inequality and Segregation in Jobs.* Toronto: Centre for Urban and Community Studies, University of Toronto, 1981.

Remnant, R. "Italian Students in Toronto Schools: Equality in Difference." *Canadian Society for the Study of Education Bulletin* 2 (September 1974): 2-7.

Ricciutelli, Luciana. "Growing Up as a Roman Catholic in an Italian Family or, How I Flushed My Virginity Down the Toilet." *Canadian Woman Studies/les cahiers de la femme* 8, no. 2 (Summer 1987): 24-26.

Ricciutelli, Luciana."Maria Minna: A 'Typical' Italian-Canadian." *Canadian Woman Studies/les cahiers de la femme* 8, no. 2 (Summer 1987): 65-67.

Richmond, Anthony H. *Aspects of the Absorption and Adaptation of Immigrants.* Canadian Immigration and Population Study. Ottawa: Information Canada, 1974. 51pp.

Richmond, Anthony H. *Ethnic Integration and Urban Renewal in Toronto.* Toronto: Copp Clark, 1973.

Richmond, Anthony H. *Ethnic Residential Segregation in Metropolitan Toronto.* Rev. ed. North York, Ontario: Institute for Behavioural Research, York University, 1980. 152 leaves.

Richmond, Anthony H. *Ethnic Variation in Family Income and Poverty in Canada.* Reprint ed. North York, Ontario: Institute for Behavioural Research, York University, 1979.

Richmond, Anthony H. "Ethnogenerational Variation in Educational Achievement." Paper presented at Elia Seminar Series in Italian-Canadian Studies, York University, North York, Ontario, 9 April 1986. 20 leaves.

Richmond, Anthony H. *Immigrants and Ethnic Groups in Metropolitan Toronto.* Reprint ed. North York, Ontario: Institute for Behavioural Research, 1969. 112 leaves. (First printed in 1967.)

Richmond, Anthony H., and Goldlust, John. *Family and Social Integration of Immigrants in Toronto*. North York, Ontario: Institute for Behavioural Research, York University, 1979.

Richmond, Anthony H., and Kalbach, Warren E. *Factors in the Adjustment of Immigrants and their Descendants*. Census Analytical Study. Ottawa: Statistics Canada, 1980. 481pp. Also available in French.

Sidlofsky, Samuel. *The Changing Urban Structure and Post-War Immigrants with Special Reference to the Toronto Italian Population*. Ottawa: Department of Manpower and Immigration, 1964.

Smith, Bruna. "Centro Femminile: A Source of Help to Immigrant Women." *Multiculturalism* 1, no. 1 (1977): 18-21.

Sturino, Franc. "Oral History in Ethnic Studies and Implications for Education." *Canadian Oral History Association Journal* 4, no. 1 (1979): 14-21.

Szado, Daniela. "The Social Roots of Wife Battering. An Examination of the Phenomenon in Mediterranean Immigrant Communities." *Canadian Woman Studies/les cahiers de la femme* 8, no. 2 (Summer 1987): 41-42.

Toscana, Silvana. "Teaching English, Italian Style." In *Education of Immigrant Students: Issues and Answers*. Symposium Series no. 5, pp. 46-51. Edited by Aaron Wolfgang. Toronto: Ontario Institute for Studies in Education, 1975.

Troper, Harold, and Palmer, Lee. *Issues in Cultural Diversity*. Canadian Critical Issues Series. Toronto: Ontario Institute for Studies in Education, 1976. Chap. 5 (St. Leonard), pp. 69-85.

Visano, Livi A. "Italo-Canadians and the Mafia: A Case of Misplaced Deviant Designations." In *Deviant Designations: Crime, Law and Deviance in Canada.* Co-edited by Livi A. Visano. Toronto: Butterworths, 1983.

Wilkinson, Derek. "Education and the Social Mobility of Three Ethnic Groups: A Canadian Case Study." In *Canadian Ethnic Studies* 13, no. 2 (1981): 61-71.

Witzel, Anne. *Italian Immigrants and Italy: An Introduction to the Multi-media Package on Italy.* Toronto: Research Department, Board of Education for the City of Toronto, 1969. 13 leaves.

Wolfgang, Aaron. "Basic Issues and Plausible Answers in Counselling New Canadians." In *Education of Immigrant Students: Issues and Answers.* Symposium Series no. 5, pp. 139-48. Edited by Aaron Wolfgang. Toronto: Ontario Institute for Studies in Education, 1975.

Wolfgang, Aaron. "Cross-Cultural Comparison of Locus of Control, Optimism toward the Future, and Time Horizon among Italian, Italo-Canadian, and New Canadian Youth." In *American Psychological Association Proceedings, 81st Annual Convention* 8 (1973): 299-300.

Wright, E.N. *Programmes Placement Related to Selected Countries of Birth and Selected Languages (Further Every Student Survey Analyses).* Report no. 99. Toronto: Research Department, Board of Education for the City of Toronto, October 1971. 31 leaves.

Wright, E.N. *Student's Background and its Relationship to Class and Programme in School (The Every Student Survey).* Report no. 91. Toronto: Research Department, Board of Education for the City of Toronto, December 1970. 61 leaves.

Wright, E.N., and McLeod, D.B. *Parents' Occupations, Student's Mother Tongue and Immigrant Status: Further Analysis of the Every Student Survey Data.* Report no. 98. Toronto: Research Department, Board of Education for the City of Toronto, September 1971; Rev. ed. December 1971. 25 leaves.

Younge, Eva R. "Population Movements and the Assimilation of Alien Groups in Canada." *Canadian Journal of Economics and Political Science* 10, no. 3 (August 1944): 372-80.

Ziegler, Suzanne. "Measuring Inter-Ethnic Attitudes in a Multi-Ethnic Context." *Canadian Ethnic Studies* 12, no. 3 (1980).

Ziegler, Suzanne. "Report from Canada: Adolescents' Inter-ethnic Friendships." *Children Today* (March-April 1980).

Ziegler, Suzanne. "School for Life: The Experience of Italian Immigrants in Canadian Schools." *Human Organization* 39, no. 3 (Fall 1980): 263-67.

Ziegler, Suzanne. "The Family Unit and International Migration: The Perceptions of Italian Immigrant Children." *International Migration Review* 2, no. 3 (Fall 1977): 326-33.

IL CONGRESSO

IL GIORNALE... DALLA COMUNITÀ ALLA COMUNITÀ.

Published Monthly by the Italians of Alberta

Second Class Mail Registration Number 6397

ANNO 3 NUMERO 5   MAY 1986 MAGGIO   9227 - 169 Ave . EDMONTON, Alberta

FORZA ITALIA

Nella foto (Ansa) : Rossi e Tardelli nel piccolo campo di Roccaraso preparato proprio per ospitare gli azzurri

Roccaraso (Ansa) - Per abituare i giocatori della nazionale di calcio italiana alla quota di Città del Messico, l'allenatore Enzo Bearzot ha portato la squadra e l'equipe tecnica a Roccaraso, la ridente cittadina dell'appennino abruzzese situata a 2000 metri di quota.

La squadra ha potuto così godere di un clima disteso, lontano da clamori e polemiche prima di affrontare i mondiali.

Relazioni Italia-Canada

PRESENTATO A ROMA IL NUMERO UNICO DEL

"VELTRO" ITALIA - CANADA

Roma - In occasione della visita ufficiale in Italia, sono stati presentati al Governatore Generale del Canada, S.E. Jeanne Sauvé, i due volumi della Rivista "IL VELTRO", dedicati alle relazioni tra l'Italia e il Canada.

I due numeri unici comprendono 60 articoli, per complessive 600 pagine, dovuti ai più competenti studiosi italiani e canadesi, che illustrano le relazioni storiche, le relazioni letterarie e artistiche, gli studi italiani in Canada e quelli canadesi in Italia, la didattica e la linguistica, le istituzioni e le iniziative , volte a una reciproca conoscenza.

I volumi del "VELTRO" sui rapporti italo-canadesi continuano la serie dei numeri speciali dedicati dalla rivista alle relazioni tra l'Italia e altri paesi o aree geografiche. La serie, iniziata nel 1950, - ora giunta alla diciassettesima pubblicazione -, ad allora occupa un posto di rilievo nell'attenzione dei lettori in Italia e all'estero.

L'importanza dell'iniziativa editoriale del "VELTRO" è del resto sottolineata dalla presenza dei messaggi dei Capi di Stato dei due Paesi: Sandro Pertini e S.E. Jeanne Suavé, che hanno evidenziato il significato delle relazioni tra l'Italia e il Canada, paese dove il contributo della comunità di origine italiana è da molti anni ormai particolarmente rilevante, anche alla luce dell'Accordo culturale italo-canadese del maggio 1984, che ai rapporti tra i due paesi darà nuovo impulso e sarà motivo di sviluppo di programmi comuni con prospettive di grande respiro.

ELEZIONI '86

di Lina Amodio

Chi l'ha chiamata rivolta, chi apatia generale, ma il risultato rimane lo stesso. Dopo quasi 20 anni il partito conservatore ha perduto quella maggioranza assoluta di seggi, che faceva dell'Alberta un'eccentricità tra le province del Canada.

Ci eravamo abituati e dormire durante l'elezione e specialmente durante il programma televisivo che annunciava i risultati. Ma giovedì 8 maggio, un brivido di gioia o di terrore (dipende dalle proprie opinioni politiche), ha pervaso tutta l'Alberta. I risultati sono stati sorprendenti: abbiamo nientedimeno 22 seggi all'opposizione. Un piccolo numero se si paragona alle altre province, ma una grande impresa se si considera che solo pochi mesi orsono questo era inconcepibile in Alberta.

Ma le cose nell'ultimo anno sono ben cambiate per il partito conservatore: Lougheed ci ha lasciato; buono per lui, quando l'economia cominciava ad andare a rotoli, il prezzo del petrolio continua a scendere e l'agricoltura è in uno stato pietoso. L'ottimismo di Getty, che tutto questo è temporaneo non ha convinto la popolazione e l'Alberta ha deciso di inviare al governo un messaggio deciso: o si decide a formulare un fermo programma per affrontare questi problemi o il PC potrà trovarsi in peggiori acque.

Ad essere colpiti principalmente da questa ondata di malcontento sono stati fra lo stupore di tutti, 6 ministri tra i più visibili del governo Getty: J.Koziak, B. Diachuk, G.Amerongen, D. King, M.LeMessurier, M.Pani. Ma la vittoria incontestata spetta al partito New Democrat, che sotto la guida di R. Martin è riuscito a portare il numero dei seggi da 2 a 16. La sua gioia è stata immensa e con un tale numero di seggi il lavoro del partito come opposizione ufficiale al governo, sarà più facile.

Ma la più grande sorpresa di quest'elezione sono stati i liberali, ci credete 4 al governo? Per il loro leader Nick Taylor questo è il segno che il partito in Alberta sta prendendo terreno e con persone come Bettie Hewes al suo fianco è facile capire il suo ottimismo.

Gli altri due seggi sono andati al partito Representative. Ma l'euforia del momento è ora seguita dalla realtà; dal duro lavoro che aspetta tutti i partiti rappresentanti.

Ma il compito più arduo è del premier; contare troppo sulle risorse naturali è stato un errore che lo stesso Lougheed non riuscì ad evitare. Getty deve cominciare a prendere importanti iniziative perché l'economia dell'Alberta cominci a diversificarsi, stimolando altri settori che non siano dipendenti dal petrolio.

Queste elezioni non sono state certo favorevoli ai nostri due connazionali nella circoscrizione di Calder.

Le nostre simpatie vanno a T.Falcone e A. Iafolla, il cui lavoro è stato senz'altro apprezzato da noi tutti.

Siamo consapevoli delle continue pressioni che avvengono durante una campagna elettorale e che litigi e battibecchi sono all'ordine del giorno; ma ci rammarica che incidenti di tal genere, che potevano essere evitati, siano accaduti anche tra di noi.

La nostra comunità ha raggiunto una maturità tale da poter pienamente partecipare alla vita politica dell'Alberta. È importante che ulteriori miglioramenti vengano effettuati per non dare adito a tali incidenti che riescono solo a nascondere le qualità dei candidati.

Speriamo che in un prossimo futuro tutto questo possa avverarsi per il successo dell'individuo e della comunità in generale.

SECTION 4: SELECTED POPULAR ACCOUNTS

"A Toronto comme à Montreal, les Italiens de vieille souche sont trés bien adaptés à la vie canadienne." *Le Magazine Macleans*, December 1961, pp. 50, 52-53.

Allen, Robert Thomas. "Portrait of Little Italy: How 160,000 Italians Are Bringing a New Flavour and Vitality to Our Staidest City." *Maclean's*, 21 March 1964, pp. 17-19, 43-44, 46.

Allen, Patrick. "Les Italo-Canadiens n'ont pas qu'un son de clocke." *L'Action Nationale*, Fevrier 1977, pp. 486-87.

Ares, Richard. "Le groupe Italien." *L'Action Nationale*, Mars 1976, pp. 439-42.

Ashwell, Mary. "Bobby's Beat ...." *Liberty*, 31 March 1964, pp. 35-36. On Bobby Curtola of Port Arthur, Ontario.

Barkway, Michael. "Drastic Check to Immigration." *Saturday Night*, 26 July 1952, pp. 15-16.

Belliveau, J.E. "How Are Canada's Italians Making Out." *The Toronto Star Weekly*, 17 March 1956.

Bodsworth, Fred. "What Kind of Canadians Are We Getting?" *Maclean's*, 15 February 1952, pp. 16-17, 34-38.

Caccia, Charles L. "Arturo Scotti." *Canadian Scene*, 30 October 1959, pp. 2-3.

de Carli, L.R. "Italo-Canadian Businessmen Organize to Encourage Trade." *Financial Post*, 24 November 1962, p. 58.

de Villiers, Marq. "Can a White Anglo-Saxon Protestant Find True Happiness in Little Italy?" *Toronto Life*, March 1968, pp. 46-47.

de Villiers, Marq. "Farewell to Little Italy." *Toronto Life*, July 1977, pp. 43-49. Includes Section, " 'La crema della crema' of the Italian Establishment."

Drea, Frank. "Lucia's Trying Love Affair With Canada." *Chatelaine*, April 1961, pp. 40-41, 61-64.

Dubro, James. *Mob Rule: Inside the Canadian Mafia.* Toronto: Macmillan, 1985. 317pp.

Dubro, James, and Rowland, Robin F. *King of the Mob.* New York: Viking, 1987. 372pp.

Ferrante, Angela. "When in Canada, Do as the Canadese Do." *Maclean's*, 6 February 1978, p. 49.

Fraser, Blair. "Can the Immigration Issue Lick the Liberals?" *Maclean's*, 10 December 1955, pp. 8, 121-22.

Fraser, Sylvia. "Laura Sabia: Not Exactly Mom and Apple Pie." *Chatelaine*, November 1975, pp. 54-55, 98-106.

Freeman, Bill, and Hewitt, Marshall, eds. *Their Town: The Mafia, the Media and the Party Machine.* Toronto: James Lorimer, 1979.

Friedmann, W.G. "Our Growing Immigration Is Everyone's Business." *Saturday Night*, 16 February 1952, pp. 12-33.

Guccione, L. "Breaking Away to the Old World." *Maclean's*, 19 January 1981, pp. 45-46, 48-49.

Harney, Robert F. "Toronto: Little Italy Now." *Attenzione*, December 1979.

Harris, Marjorie. *Toronto: The City of Neighbourhoods*. Toronto: McClelland & Stewart, 1984, pp. 26-41.

Histoire des Italiens au Québec. Illustrée par leurs enfants. Montreal: Pro-Developpement Italo-Canadien, 1982.

"How Immigrants Become Canadians All on Their Own." *Financial Post*, 22 February 1964, p. 29.

Iannucci, Amilcare A. "The Italian Immigrant: Voyage of No Return." *Canadian Forum*, March 1977, pp. 12-15.

Iannucci, Amilcare A. "The Pot Thickens ... and the Mosaic Cracks." *Books in Canada*, March 1978, pp. 9-10. Issue includes relevant comments by others.

Intscher, Janet. "Italian Connection" and "Little Italy." *Canadian Heritage*, October 1981, pp. 22-24.

"Italia Mia: Italy Is Alive and Well and Living in Centretown." *Ottawa Magazine*, July 1985, pp. 14-17.

"Italian Immigrants: Integration through Education." *Industrial Canada* 64, no. 10 (February 1964): 42-45.

"Italian Professor Joins Faculty at York." *Canadian Scene*, issue 671, 15 April 1965, pp. 6-7.

"Italians in Montreal. Writers of the New World." *Montreal Calen*, April 1985, pp. 10-11.

Jamieson, Robert. "Does Canada Really Want Immigrants?" *Saturday Night*, 23 May 1959, pp. 22-24.

Johnson, Valerie. "Our Isolated Immigrants." *Saturday Night*, February 1971, pp. 16-20.

Kahn, E.J. "Profiles: Guy Lombardo." *New Yorker*, 5 January 1957, pp. 35-36; 12 January 1957, pp. 35-36.

Lauzon, Adèle. "190,000 Italiens resistent mal a l'exploitation." *Le Magazine Macleans*, December 1961, pp. 20-22, 48.

Lenoir, Gaston. "Italy in Toronto." *Toronto Calendar Magazine* 6, no. 2 (1974): 36-43.

"Life in Canada Enriched by Flood of Immigrants." *Financial Post*, 24 November 1962.

Macfarlane, David. "Stations of the Heart." *Saturday Night*, April 1987, pp. 44-50. On Toronto's Little Italy.

MacInnis, Grace. "Immigration? On What Basis?" *Canadian Forum*, April 1947, pp. 7-8.

McQueen, Rod. "The New Italian Super-Rich." *Toronto Life*, December 1985, pp. 36-39, 67-76.

"Montreal Italian Writers. Quebec's Third Solitude." *Quill and Quire*, March 1985, p. 60.

Morse, Larry. "Exploring the City. St. Clair West." *Toronto Life*, November 1984, pp. 74-75.

Navone, John J. "Canada's Immigration Problems." *America* 103 (April 1960): 106-10.

Paquet, J. Claude. "Les Italiens de Montréal." *La Presse Magazine*, 25 janvier 1964, pp. 3-5.

Peterson, Virgil. *The Mob*. Ottawa: Green Hill Publishers, 1983.

Rasky, Frank. "Italian New Canadians: Our Gayest Neighbours." *Liberty*, June 1958, pp. 16-17, 48-54.

"The Realm: Immigration Showdown." *Time*, 23 May 1955, p. 36.

Robert, Marika. "Che bella. The Old-World Pleasure Garden Comes to the Suburbs." *Maclean's*, 23 September 1961, pp. 24-25, 43-45.

Russell, George. "The Italians in Canada: Builders of a New Life." *Weekend Magazine*, 5 October 1974, pp. 7-16.

Salutin, Rick. "World Cup." *This Magazine* 16, no. 5 (November 1982), p. 26.

Taylor, Rupert J. "Discoverers and City Dwellers. The Italians." *Canada and the World*, September 1976, p. 22.

Trevor, Chris. "Josephine's Story." *Canadian Labour* 7, no. 6 (June 1962): 9-10.

West, Bruce. *Toronto*. The Romance of Canadian Cities Series. Toronto: Doubleday, 1967; reprint ed. 1979, pp. 227, 260-61, 270.

Wismer, Catherine. *Sweethearts*. Toronto: James Lorimer, 1980. 222pp. Re "mob" activity in building trades.

Italian Canadians in peace demonstration, Toronto, 1987. Courtesy Roger Hollander

SECTION 5: THESES

Aasen, Clarence T. "Ethnicity, Politics and Urban Planning: Political Uses of French and Italian Ethnicity in Two Local Area Planning Processes." Ph.D. diss., University of Waterloo, 1980.

Barrett, Frank Alexander. "Post-War European Immigrants in Metropolitan Toronto. M.A. diss., University of Minnesota, 1963. Chap. 2(1) Italians.

Bayley, Charles M. "The Social Structure of the Italian and Ukrainian Immigrant Communities in Montreal, 1935-1937." M.A. diss., McGill University, 1939.

Bertrand, Michele. "Repartition des groupes ethniques sur l'île de Montréal d'après les circonscriptions électorales fédérales du recensement de 1961." B. arch., Université de Montréal, 1966.

Binns, Margaret A. "Cultural Pluralism in Canada; An Exploratory Study of the Italians and Ukrainians in London, Ontario." M.A. diss., University of Western Ontario, 1971.

Brandino, Diana. "The Italians in Hamilton, 1921-1946." M.A. diss., University of Western Ontario, 1977.

Buckley, Patricia Lorraine. "A Cross Cultural Study of Drinking Patterns in Three Ethnic Groups: Coast Salish Indians of the Mission Reserve, Immigrant Italians and Anglo-Saxons of East Vancouver." M.A. diss., University of British Columbia, 1968.

Canzona, Lino. "Employment Factors Affecting the Integration of Immigrant Families: a Comparative Study of the Adjustment of British, German, Hungarian and Italian Immigrant Husbands in the Economic Life of Canada." M.S.W. diss., University of Toronto, 1964.

Castellano, V. "Mental Illness among Italian Immigrants." M.S.W. diss., University of Toronto, 1959.

Castelli, G. " 'La sosta dello spirito.' Autocritique. Relance d'une rubrique de caractère religieux en langue italienne au Poste de Radio C.F.M.B. à Montréal." M.A. diss., Université de Montréal, 1979.

Ciccocelli, Joseph Anthony. "The Innocuous Enemy Alien: Italians in Canada during World War II." M.A. diss., University of Western Ontario, 1977.

Colalillo, Giuliana. "Culture conflict in the adolescent Italian girl." M.A. diss., University of Toronto, 1974.

Colalillo, Giuliana. "Value Structures Within Italian Immigrant Families: Continuity or Conflict?" Ph.D. diss., University of Toronto.

Craig, Jean Carol. "Associations of Persons of Italian Origin in Toronto." M.A. diss., University of Toronto, 1957.

Elliott, Una. "Comparative Roles of the People of Italian and Netherlandish Origin in the Creation of a Homogeneous Population in the City of London." M.A. diss., University of Western Ontario, 1964.

Fallico, Maria. "La sindrome dell'emigrato: cambiamento culturale e condizionamento sociali a S. Vincenzo La Costa. Indagine su un campione di lettere di emigrati ai familiari." Diss., Università degli Studi della Calabria, 1982.

Fainella, John G. "Cultural Background and Italian Settlement in Calgary." M.A. diss., University of Calgary, 1975.

Fenton, Charles Stephen. "Assimilation Processes among Immigrants: a Study of German and Italian Immigrants to Hamilton." M.A. diss., McMaster University, 1968.

Ferraris, Mary. "Factors Influencing the Integration of a Group of Italian Women Immigrants in Toronto." M.A. diss., York University, 1969. 209 leaves (fische).

Feuerverger, Grace. "An Exploratory Study of the Ethnolinguistic Vitality of Italo-Canadian Students in Toronto." M.A. diss., University of Toronto, 1982.

Kydd, Mary Winnifred. "Alien Races in the Canadian West." M.A. diss., McGill University, 1924.

Kolcon-Lach, Emilia. "The History of the Pre-1920 Italian Settlement at Sault Ste. Marie, Ontario." M.A. diss., University of Western Ontario, 1979.

Langdon, Susan Jane. "Educational and Occupational Mobility of Young Italians: a Case Study." M.A. diss., University of Guelph, 1977.

Marjoribanks, Kevin McLeod. "Ethnic and Environmental Influence on Levels and Profiles of Mental Abilities." Ph.D. diss., University of Toronto, 1970.

Meleg, M.S. "Italian and Ukrainian University Students' View of Occupations in Canada: a Study of the Relationship between Ethnicity and Occupational Prestige." M.A. diss., University of Windsor, 1968.

Novak, Carole. "Intellectual Assessment of the Bilingual Italian Immigrant Children in their Native Language." M.A. diss., University of Toronto, 1973.

Parry, Harriet J. Anderson. "The 'Black Widows' of the Mediterranean." M.A. diss., York University, 1977.

Peressini, Mauro. "Pratiques et stratégies migratoires: le cas des Italiens originaires du Frioul." M.A. diss., Université de Montréal, 1983.

Philpott, Stuart Bowman. "Trade Unionism and Acculturation, a Comparative Study of Urban Indians and Immigrant Italians." M.A. diss., University of British Columbia, 1963.

Potestio, John. "From Navvies to Contractors: the History of Vincenzo and Giovanni Veltri, Founders of the R.F. Welch Limited, 1885-1931." M.A. diss., Lakehead University, 1982.

Pucci, Antonio. "The Italian Community in Fort William's East End in the Early Twentieth Century." M.A. diss., Lakehead University, 1977.

Rees-Powell, Alan Thomas. "Differentials in the Integration Process of Dutch and Italian Immigrants in Edmonton." M.S.W. diss., University of Alberta, 1964.

Ribordy, Francois-Xavier. "Conflit de culture et criminalité des Italiens à Montréal." Ph.D. diss., University of Montreal, 1970.

Scrutton, R. Edgar. "Intergenerational Conflicts in the Italian Families, Amherstburg, Ontario: a Study of Mother-Daughter Responses." M.A. diss., University of Windsor, 1978.

Sidlofsky, Samuel. "Post-War Immigrants in the Changing Metropolis – With Special Reference to Toronto's Italian Population." 2 vols. Ph.D. diss., University of Toronto, 1969.

Snider, Howard Mervin. "Variables Affecting Immigrant Adjustment: A Study of Italians in Edmonton." M.A. diss., University of Alberta, 1966.

Sturino, Franc. "Inside the Chain: A Case Study in Southern Italian Migration to North America, 1880-1930." 2 vols. Ph.D. diss., University of Toronto, 1981.

Taschereau, Sylvie. "Pays et Patries: mariages et lieux d'origine des Italiens de Montréal, 1906-1930." M.A. diss., Université du Québec à Montréal, 1984.

Velloni, Pietro. "Les immigrants italiens à Québec." M.A. diss., Laval University, 1961.

Venditti, Mario P. "The Italian Ethnic Community of Metropolitan Toronto: A Case Study in Intra-Urban Migration." M.A. research paper, York University, 1975.

Vincent, Patrick. "The Assimilation Process: with Special Reference to Italian Children in the Hamilton School System." M.A. diss., McMaster University, 1968.

Willman, Pamela M. "Leisure Time for the First Generation Italians in Vancouver, 1965-66." M.S.W. diss., University of British Columbia, 1966.

Ziegler, Suzanne Gross. "The Adaptation of Italian Immigrants to Toronto: An Analysis." Ph.D. diss., University of Colorado, 1971.

Zucchi, John. "The Development of Italian National Identity among Toronto's Italian Immigrants." Ph.D. diss., University of Toronto, 1983.

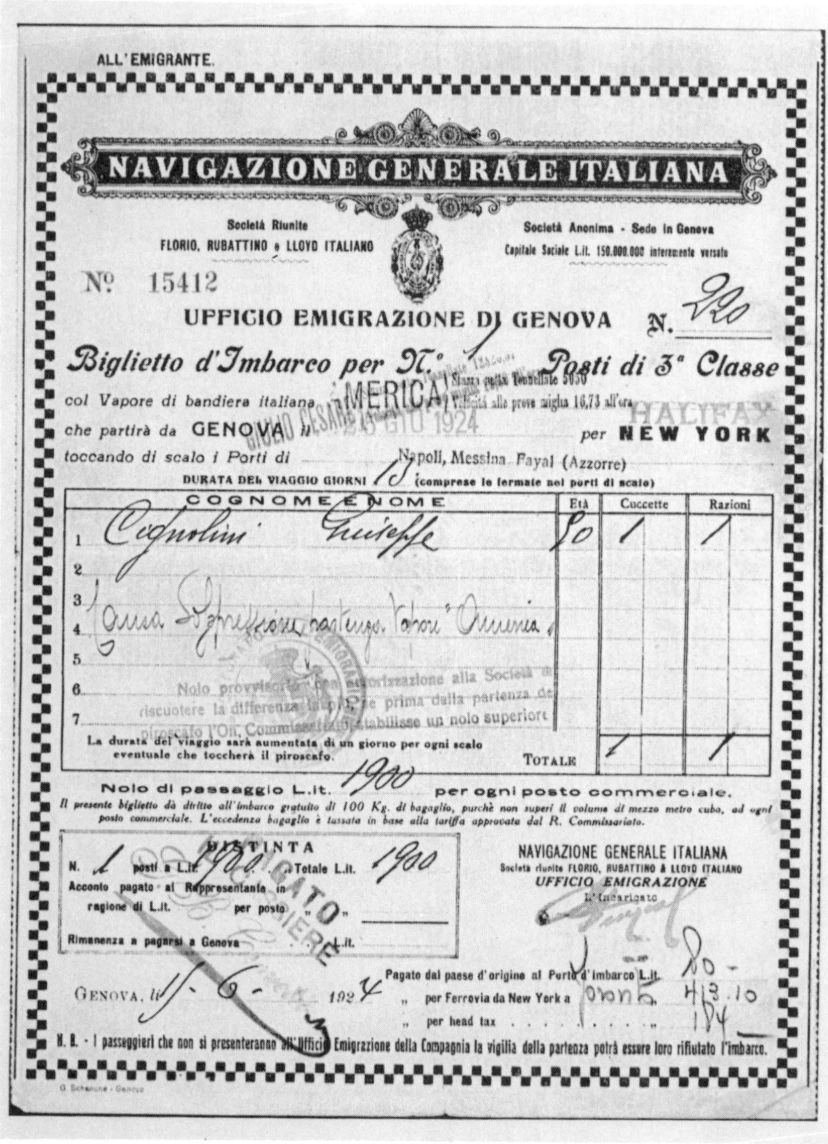
ALL'EMIGRANTE.

NAVIGAZIONE GENERALE ITALIANA

Società Riunite FLORIO, RUBATTINO e LLOYD ITALIANO

Società Anonima - Sede in Genova
Capitale Sociale L.it. 150.000.000 interamente versato

N° 15412

UFFICIO EMIGRAZIONE DI GENOVA N. 920

Biglietto d'Imbarco per N.° 1 Posti di 3ª Classe

col Vapore di bandiera italiana "MERICA" ... Velocità alle prove miglia 16,73 all'ora

che partirà da GENOVA il 25 GIU 1924 per NEW YORK

toccando di scalo i Porti di Napoli, Messina, Fayal (Azzorre)

DURATA DEL VIAGGIO GIORNI 13 (comprese le fermate nei porti di scalo)

	COGNOME E NOME	Età	Cuccette	Razioni
1	Cognolini Giuseppe	80	1	1
2				
3				
4				
5				
6	Nolo provvisorio con autorizzazione alla Società di			
7	riscuotere la differenza ... prima della partenza del piroscafo l'On. Commissariato stabilisse un nolo superiore			
	La durata del viaggio sarà aumentata di un giorno per ogni scalo eventuale che toccherà il piroscafo.	TOTALE	1	1

Nolo di passaggio L.it. 1900 per ogni posto commerciale.

Il presente biglietto dà diritto all'imbarco gratuito di 100 Kg. di bagaglio, purchè non superi il volume di mezzo metro cubo, ad ogni posto commerciale. L'eccedenza bagaglio è tassata in base alla tariffa approvata dal R. Commissariato.

DISTINTA

N. 1 posti a L.it. 1900 Totale L.it. 1900

Acconto pagato al Rappresentante in ragione di L.it. per posto " "

Rimanenza a pagarsi a Genova L.it.

PAGATO CASSIERE

NAVIGAZIONE GENERALE ITALIANA
Società riunite FLORIO, RUBATTINO & LLOYD ITALIANO
UFFICIO EMIGRAZIONE
L'Incaricato

GENOVA, li 15-6- 1924

Pagato dal paese d'origine al Porto d'imbarco L.it. 80 -
" per Ferrovia da New York a Toronto 43.10
" per head tax 184

N. B. - I passeggieri che non si presenteranno all'Ufficio Emigrazione della Compagnia la vigilia della partenza potrà essere loro rifiutato l'imbarco.

G. Schenone - Genova

Italian boarding certificate, 1924

SECTION 6: SOURCES FROM THE *BOLLETTINO DELL'EMIGRAZIONE*, 1902-27*

"Avvertenze agli emigranti italiani relative ad alcuni paesi esteri: Masiglia, Francoforte, Distretto di Fiume, Dalmazia, Rumania, Egitto, Africa del Sud, Brasile, Florida (Stati Uniti), emigrazione agli Stati Uniti per la via del Canada." No. 4, 1902, pp. 71-76.

"L'immigrazione nel Canada durante l'anno 1901." No. 9, 1902, pp. 36-40.

"Avvertenze agli emigranti italiani intorno ad alcuni paesi esteri (Stati Uniti, Canada, Transvaal, Bulgaria, Grecia)." No. 11, 1902, pp. 56-62.

"Avvertenze agli emigranti italiani intorno ad alcuni paesi esteri." No. 12, 1902, pp. 74-81.

Rossi, Egisto. "Delle condizioni del Canada rispetto all'immigrazione italiana." No. 4, 1903, pp. 3-28.

"Canada – L'immigrazione nell'anno 1902." No. 7, 1903, pp. 49-50.

"Avvertenze agli emigranti italiani intorno ad alcuni paesi esteri: Canada, Pennsylvania, Nicaragua, Paraguay, Tunisia, Bosnia-Erzegovina, Austria." No. 5, 1904, pp. 57-59.

---

* Published by the Commissariato Generale dell'Emigrazione under the auspices of the Ministero degli Affari Esteri. Listing is by date rather than alphabetical. Entries are derived from Francesco Cordasco's bibliographical guide to the *Bollettino*, cited in Section 7.

"Notizie statistiche sui movimenti migratori: L'emigrazione italiana nel 1905. – L'immigrazione nel Canada nel 1904-1905." No. 1, 1906, pp. 39-44.

"Avvertenze agli emigranti italiani intorno ad alcuni paesi esteri: Svizzera, Austria-Ungheria, Bulgaria, Malta, Egitto, Nuova York, Canada, Siria, Cina, Giappone, Svizzera." No. 5, 1906, pp. 72-78.

"Gli stranieri nel Canada guidicati da un canadese (Recensione)." No. 19, 1909, pp. 56-75.

"Legislazione sull'emigrazione e sull'immigrazione: Legge del Canada relativa all'immigrazione e agli immigrati." No. 19, 1909, pp. 3-40.

"Notizie statistiche sui movimenti migratori: L'immigrazione nel Canada secondo le statistiche canadesi." No. 19, 1909, pp. 41-55.

"Avvertenze agli emigranti intorno ad alcuni paesi esteri: Canada." No. 5, 1910, pp. 79-80.

"Lavori della Commissioni federale per l'immigrazione negli Stati Uniti: (d) Immigrazione del Canada. No. 7, 1910, pp. 10-41.

"Ispezione ai campi di lavoro di La Tuque (Canada)." No. 13, 1910, pp. 24-31.

"Le condizione degli operai italiani del distretto minerario di Cobalt, nella provincia di Ontario." No. 13, 1910, pp. 12-23.

"Notizie statistiche sui movimenti migratori. L'immigrazione nel Canada nell'anno fiscale 1908-1909." No. 13, 1910, pp. 32-58.

"Avvertenze agli emigranti italiani intorno ad alcuni paesi
esteri: Canada, Stati Uniti." No. 5, 1911, pp. 109-10.

"Canada: Regolamento che modifica temporaneamente le
disposizioni concernente la somma di cui gli immigranti
devono essere in possesso per entrare nel Canada." No. 1,
1912, pp. 25-26.

"Leggi decreti regolamenti e relazioni ufficiali sull'
immigrazione e sulla distribuzione delle terre nel
Canada." No. 2, 1912, pp. 3-269.

"L'agricoltura e l'immigrazione nel Canada." No. 5, 1912, pp.
3-36.

"Descrizione dei terreni della 'Western Prairie' Canadese."
No. 5, 1912, pp. 37-51.

"Quadri statistici relativi all'immigrazione Canadese." No. 7,
1912, pp. 7-84.

Attolico, Bernardo. "Sui campi di lavoro della nuova ferrovia
transcontinentale canadese." No. 1, 1913, pp. 3-26.

"Informazione sulle condizioni dell'emigrazione nella
provincia di Ontario." No. 14, 1913, pp. 73-74.

"La colonia italiana in Sault Ste. Marie (Ontario, Canada)."
No. 4, 1914, pp. 83-86.

"Condizioni attuali della colonia italiana in Guelph (Ontario,
Canada)." No. 4, 1914, pp. 82-83.

"Colonie italiane nel Sud Ontario tra Montreal e
Toronto, e tra Toronto e Parry Sound (Canada)." No. 6,
1914, pp. 57-79.

"Leggi sul lavoro nella provincia di Saskatchewan (Canada)."
   No. 6, 1914, p. 60.

"Mercato del lavoro in Canada nel primo Trimestre 1914." No.
   6, 1914, pp. 60-61.

"La disciplina dell'immigrazione secondo le legge canadesi
   specialmente a confronto con la legislazione degli Stati
   Uniti e nei rapporti con Italia." No. 7, 1914, pp. 3-314.

"La disciplina dell'immigrazione secondo le legge canadesi,
   specialmente a confronto la legislazione degli Stati Uniti e
   nei rapporti con Italia." No. 8, 1914, pp. 3-161.

Moroni, Gerolamo. "Le condizione attuali dei lavori sulla
   grande transcontinentale del Canada." No. 9, 1914, pp. 45-
   50.

"Atti Ufficiali del Ministero degli Affari Esteri e del
   Commissariato dell'emigrazione: Infortuni sul lavoro
   avvenuti nel Canada durante il primo semestre dell'anno
   1914." No. 13, 1914, p. 69.

"Emigranti italiani arrivati in Canada durante il trimestre
   luglio - settembre 1914." No. 13, 1914, p. 68.

Moroni, Girolamo. "Il British Columbia." No. 1, 1915, pp. 67-
   79.

"Dati statistici sull'emigrazione in Canada durante il periodo
   1°, aprile 1913-marzo 1914." No. 2, 1915, pp. 113-15.

Moroni, Girolamo. "La Regione delle provincie centrali del
   Canada." No. 2, 1915, pp. 41-71.

Statistiche degli infortuni sul lavoro nel Canada (semestre
   luglio - dicembre 1914)." No. 2, 1915, pp. 115-16.

Moroni, Gerolamo. "Norme per la concessione o vendita dei terreni, a scope agricola, nel Canada." No. 3, 1915, pp. 69-78.

Moroni, Girolamo. "Immigrazione al Canada nell'anno fiscale 1913-1914." No. 5, 1915, pp. 52-56.

Moroni, Girolamo. "La provincia di Quebec (Canada)." No. 5, 1915, pp. 42-51.

Moroni, Girolamo. "La provincia dell' Ontario." No. 6, 1915, pp. 47-82.

Moroni, Girolamo. "Le provincie marittime del Canada." No. 7, 1915, pp. 63-78.

"Canada: La protezione del lavoro e le donne di servizio." No. 7, 1916, p. 89.

"Canada: Politica immigratoria." No. 3, 1919, pp. 42-43.

"Canada: Uffici di collocamento." No. 3, 1919, pp. 43-45.

"Canada: Condizioni dell'emigrazione e del lavoro." Nos. 1-3, 1920, pp. 51-62.

"Canada: Conferenza sulla immigrazione delle donne." Nos. 1-3, 1920, pp. 62-63.

"Canada: Emendamendo alla legge sugli infortuni del lavoro nella provincia di Alberta." Nos. 1-3, 1920, pp. 49-51.

"Canada: Immigrazione nell'anno 1919." Nos. 4 & 5, 1920, pp. 169-70.

"Canada: Regolamento 24 dicembre 1919, che modifica le disposizioni concernente la somma di cui devono essere in possesso gli immigranti." Nos. 4 & 5, 1920, p. 150.

"Canada: Condizioni generali del lavoro della immigrazione."
No. 6, 1920, pp. 235-38.

"Canada: Legislazione sociale." Nos. 8-9, 1920, pp. 409-10.

"Canada: Condizioni del lavoro e della emigrazione nella
provincia di Alberta nel 1° semestre 1920. Nos. 10-12,
1920, pp. 499-502.

"Canada: Movimento immigratorio nel 1° semestre 1920."
Nos. 10-12, 1920, pp. 498-99.

"Canada: Il Congresso del Lavoro e la disciplina
dell'emigrazione." No. 1, 1921, p. 45.

"Canada: Immigrazione e colonizzazione nel 3° trimestre
1920." No. 1, 1921, pp. 45-47.

"Canada: Per gli emigranti diretti al Canada." No. 1, 1921, pp.
44-45.

"Canada: Scioperi in Canada durante il mese di settembre
1920." No. 1, 1921, p. 47.

"Canada: I prezzi dei terreni in Canada. No. 2, 1921, p. 95.

"Canada: La distribuzione delle terre agli ex-combattenti."
No. 2, 1921, p. 95.

"Canada: Collocamento e controllo sull' immigrazione." No. 4,
1921, pp. 239-41.

"Canada: Condizioni per l'emigrazione." No. 4, 1921, p. 239.

"Canada: Ordinanza P.C. 959, 19 marzo 1921, che proroga a
tempo indeterminato le disposizioni relative alla somma di
cui gli emigranti devono essere in possesso per entrare nel
Canada." No. 5, 1921, p. 324.

"Canada: I salari minimi per gli operai." Nos. 6 & 7, 1921, p. 406.

"Canada: Ordinanza 26 luglio 1921 (P.C. 2669) concernente il visto ai passaporti per l'entrata nel Canada." Nos. 11 & 12, 1921, p. 751.

"Canada: Ordinanza 26 luglio 1921 (P.C. 2668) che determina la scorta minima di denaro di cui devono essere forniti gli immigranti per essere ammessi nel Canada." Nos. 11 & 12, 1921, pp. 750-51.

"Canada: La immigrazione nel Canada nel periodo gennaio-settembre 1921." No. 1, 1922, pp. 23-24.

"Canada: L'immigrazione nel 1921." No. 5, 1922, p. 345.

"Canada: Ordinanza in Consiglio 9 maggio 1922 (P.C. 715) con la quale vengono stabiliti nuove norme sull' immigrazione." No. 6, 1922, pp. 445-46.

"Canada: Immigrazione nel primo trimestre del 1922." No. 7, 1922, p. 524.

"Canada: L'immigrazione dei giovani nel Canada." No. 9, 1922, pp. 687-88.

"Canada: Progetti di colonizzazione." Nos. 10-12, 1922, pp. 784-85.

"Canada: Disoccupazione." Nos. 1 & 2, 1923, pp. 24-25.

"Canada: Scioperi." Nos. 1 & 2, 1923, p. 25.

"Canada: Trattoto di commercio con l'Italia." No. 3, 1923, pp. 130-31.

"Canada: Demografia ed immigrazione." No. 4, 1923, pp. 237-38.

"Canada: Disoccupazione." No. 4, 1923, p. 237.

"Canada: Disposizioni sull'immigrazione." No. 4, 1923, p. 238.

"Canada: Scioperi." No. 4, 1923, p. 237.

"Canada: L'emigrazione dal primo gennaio al 31 dicembre 1922." No. 6, 1923, pp. 443-44.

"Canada: Il programma del Governo per l'immigrazione." No. 6, 1923, pp. 444-45.

"Canada: Mercato del lavoro durante il 1922." No. 6, 1923, pp. 445-46.

"Canada: Nota ai dati statistici: L'emigrazione italiana nel secondo bimestre 1923." No. 6, 1923, pp. 463-65.

"Canada; Ordinanza di Consiglio del 31 gennaio 1923, con la quale vengono stabilite nuove norme sull'emigrazione." No. 6, 1923, pp. 453-54.

"Canada: Stranieri ammissibili nel Canada." No. 6, 1923, p. 443.

"Canada: Emendamento alla legge sui conflitti del lavoro." No. 7, 1923, p. 557.

"Canada: La colonizzazione straniera al Canada e la politica immigratoria del Governo." No. 2, 1924, pp. 28-31.

"Canada: Nuove disposizioni sulle pensioni." No. 2, 1924, pp. 124-25.

"Canada: Politica immigratoria." No. 2, 1924, pp. 125-26.

"Canada: Notizie sulla colonizzazione." No. 3, 1924, pp. 204-05.

"Canada: L'organizzazione del mercato della mano d'opera."
No. 4, 1924, pp. 312-14.

"Canada: Collocamento e assistenza di coloni inglesi." No. 5,
1924, p. 410.

"Canada: La legislazione sociale nel 1923." No. 5, 1924, pp.
409-10.

"Canada: La colonizzazione del Manitoba." Nos. 7 & 8, 1924, p.
616.

"Canada: L'esodo degli operai canadesi per gli Stati Uniti.
Nos. 7 & 8, 1924, pp. 616-17.

"Canada: L'immigrazione nel secondo trimestre del 1924." No.
11, 1924, p. 925.

"Canada: L'immigrazione nel secondo trimestre del 1924." No.
1, 1925, p. 30.

"Canada: La mano d'opera orientale." No. 3, 1925, p. 264.

"Canada: Una colonia agricola italiana." No. 7, 1925, pp. 704-
05.

"Canada: I servizi d'immigrazione." No. 12, 1925, p. 1279.

"Canada: L'immigrazione." No. 12, 1925, p. 1279.

"Canada: Manifestazioni italo-canadese a Ottawa." No. 3,
1926, p. 244.

"Canada: Legge sulla pensione per vecchiaia." No. 5, 1926, pp.
520-21.

"Canada: Un progetto del Governo canadese per l'istituzione
di una Cassa di prestito ai coloni. No. 5, 1926, pp. 517-20.

"Canada: L'immigrazione." No. 6, 1926, pp. 697-98.

"Canada: Collocamento e disoccupazione." No. 8, 1926, pp. 992-93.

"Canada: Costo della vita." No. 8, 1926, p. 993.

"Canada: L'immigrazione." No. 8, 1926, pp. 991-92.

"Canada: La pensione per la vecchiaia." No. 8, 1926, p. 992.

"Canada: La politica del Governo verso l'immigrazione straniera." No. 8, 1926, p. 992.

"Canada: Lavoratori inglesi e lavoratori stranieri." No. 9, 1926, pp. 1167-69.

"Canada: Colonizzazione britannica." No. 12, 1926, p. 1533.

"Canada: Gli immigranti europei." No. 12, 1926, p. 1953.

"Canada: Per la colonizzazione." No. 12, 1926, p. 1534.

"Canada: Richiamare i canadesi emigrati." No. 12, 1926, pp. 1953-54.

"Gli Italiani nel Mondo: Canada." No. 2, 1927, p. 208.

"Canada: Richieste del lavoro sindacato in materia di emigrazione." No. 3, 1927, pp. 338-39.

"Canada: L'immigrazione nel primo quarto di secolo." No. 4, 1927, pp. 490-94.

"Italia: Accordi amministrative Italo-Canadese sull' emigrazione." No. 4, 1927, p. 468.

"Canada: Gli italiani nella provincia dell'Ontario." No. 5, 1927, pp. 678-80.

"Canada: I salari agricola." No. 5, 1927, pp. 650-52.

"Canada: La vaccinazione degli emigranti." No. 5, 1927, p. 652.

"Canada: L'immigrazione svizzera." No. 6, 1927, pp. 813-14.

"Canada: L'importanza dello sbocco immigratorio canadese." No. 6, 1927, p. 813.

"Canada: Protesta contro l'immigrazione non britannica." No. 6, 1927, p. 814.

"Canada: Un accordo provvisorio per l'immigrazione polacca al Canada." No. 6, 1927, p. 813.

"Canada: Agricoltura ed immigrazione." No. 7, 1927, pp. 985-86.

"Canada: In onore di Giovanni Caboto." No. 7, 1927, pp. 1007-09. Contains letters by Benito Mussolini and William Lyon Mackenzie King.

"Notizie sulla emigrazione sul lavoro: Perché l'emigrazione inglese aumenta nel Canada e nell'Australia." No. 7, 1927, pp. 963-72.

"Canada: Per l'emigrazione inglese." No. 8, 1927, pp. 1193-94.

"Segnalazioni dall'Estero: La colonizzazione al Canada." No. 8, 1927, pp. 1217-22.

"Canada: L'emigrazione dei giovani agricoltori britannici." No. 9, 1927, pp. 1400-02.

"Canada: L'avvicendamento della mano d'opera nell' industria forestale nell'Ontario." No. 10, 1927, pp. 1598-99.

"Canada: Il Congresso generale dei Sindacati del Canada." No. 10, 1927, pp. 1597-98.

"Canada: L'esempio australiano." No. 10, 1927, p. 1596.

"Canada: Il livello di vita degli operai al Canada e negli Stati Uniti." No. 10, 1927, pp. 1600-01.

"Canada: La nazionalità dei minatori nella Columbia Britannica." No. 10, 1927, pp. 1599-1600.

"Canada: Il sesto Congresso della Confederazione dei lavoratori cattolici canadesi." No. 10, 1927, pp. 1596-97.

"Canada: Vista medica degli emigranti prima della partenza." No. 10, 1927, p. 1597.

"Canada: La questione dell'immigrazione." No. 11, 1927, p. 1788.

"Canada: Gli immigranti europei." No. 12, 1927, p. 1953.

"Canada: Richiamare i canadesi emigrati." No. 12, 1927, pp. 1953-54.

THE
CASORSO
STORY

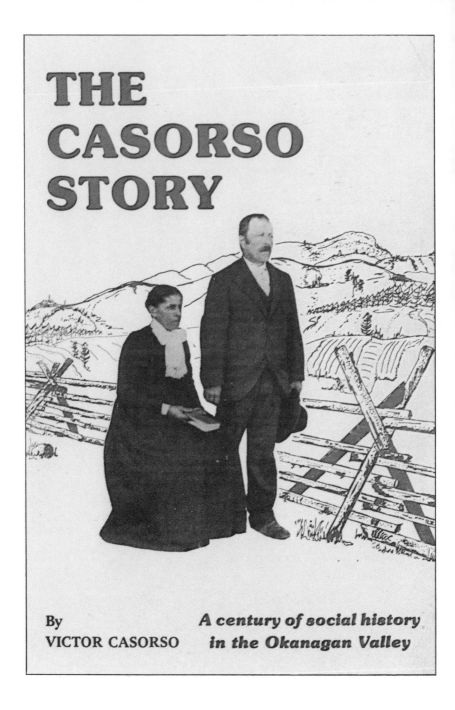

By
VICTOR CASORSO

A century of social history
in the Okanagan Valley

SECTION 7: BIBLIOGRAPHIES AND BIBLIOGRAPHICAL SOURCES

Abraham, Diana. *Cross-Cultural Social Work in Canada: An Annotated Bibliography.* Toronto: North York Interagency Council (Multicultural Workers' Network), 1980. 43pp.

Association of Canadian Community Colleges. *Communique: Canadian Studies* 3, no. 1 (October 1976). 65pp. Bibliography on multiculturalism.

Barton, Josef J. *Brief Ethnic Bibliography: An Annotated Guide to the Ethnic Experience in the United States.* Cambridge, Mass., 1976. 52pp.

Bianchini, Luciano. "University Research on Italian Canadians: A preliminary checklist." *Canadian Ethnic Studies* 2, no. 1 (1970): 117-19.

Bianchini, Luciano, and Malycky, Alexander. "Italian-Canadian Periodical Publications: A Preliminary Check List." *Canadian Ethnic Studies* 2, no. 1 (June 1970): 121-26.

Bianchini, Luciano, and Malycky, Alexander. "Italian-Canadian Periodical Publications: First Supplement." *Canadian Ethnic Studies* 5, nos. 1-2 (1973): 197-204.

Bogusis, Ruth, Blazek, Liba, and Sonnemann, Sabine. *Checklist of Canadian Ethnic Series.* Ottawa: Newspaper Division, National Library of Canada, 1981, pp. 175-89.

Briani, Vittorio. *Italian Immigrants Abroad: A Bibliography on the Italian Experience Outside of Italy, in Europe, the*

Americas, Australia and Africa. Detroit: B. Ethbridge Books, 1979. 229pp.

Buchignani, Norman. "Canadian Ethnic Research and Multiculturalism." *Journal of Canadian Studies* 17, no. 1 (Spring 1982): 16-34.

Canada. Department of Citizenship and Immigration. *Citizenship, Immigration and Ethnic Groups in Canada: A Bibliography of Research (published & unpublished sources) 1920-58.* Ottawa: Economic and Social Research Division, Department of Citizenship and Immigration, 1960. 215pp. Updates printed for 1959-61 and 1962-64.

The Canadian Encyclopedia. 1985. S.v. "Italian Writing," by Joseph Pivato. In Vol. 2, pp. 907-08.

Canadian Ethnic Studies. Volumes 1969 to 1987. Journal has regular bibliographic sections on Canadian ethnocultural themes.

The Canadian Newspaper Directory (subsequently renamed) *McKim's Directory of Canadian Publications.* Montreal, Quebec: A. McKim, editions for 1913, 1919, 1924, 1929, 1932, 1939 and 1941 regarding Italians.

Caroli, Betty Boyd. "Italian Women in America: Sources for Study." *Italian Americana* 2, no. 2 (Spring 1976): 24-36.

Cordasco, Francesco. *Italian Americans: A Guide to Information Sources.* Detroit: Gale Research, 1978. 222pp.

Cordasco, Francesco. *Italian Mass Emigration: The Exodus of a Latin People: A Bibliographical Guide to the Bollettino dell'Emigrazione 1902-1927.* Totowa, New Jersey: Rowman & Littlefield, 1980. 307pp.

della Cava, Olha. "Italian American Studies: A Progress Report." In *Perspectives in Italian Immigration and*

Ethnicity, pp. 165-72. Edited by Silvano M. Tomasi. New York: Center for Migration Studies, 1977.

della Cava, Ralph S. *Resources for the Study of Italian Emigration: A Directory of Libraries and Archives in Rome and Florence*. New York: Center for Migration Studies, 1977. 6 leaves.

Del Negro, Piero. "Per una bibliografia italo-canadese. Il Canada nella pubblicistica italiana dell'eta moderna." In *Canadiana*. Vol. 3: *Problemi di storia canadese*, pp. 13-31. Edited by Luca Codignota. Venice: Marsilio Editori, 1983.

Di Giovanni, Caroline. "Italian Canadian Writers in Ontario: The Function of Place." *Italian Canadiana* 2, no. 1 (Spring 1986): 98-107.

Di Giovanni, Caroline Morgan, ed. *Italian Canadian Voices: An Anthology of Poetry and Prose (1946-1983)*. Oakville: Mosaic and Canadian Centre for Italian Culture and Education, 1984. 205pp.

Dore, Grazia. *Bibliografia per la storia dell'emigrazione italiana in America*. Rome: Tipografia del Ministero Degli Affari Esteri, 1956. 125pp.

Edwards, Caterina. "Discovering Voice: The Second Generation Finds its Place: A Polemic." *Italian Canadiana* 2, no. 1 (Spring 1986): 63-67.

Gans, Herbert J. "Some Comments on the History of Italian Migration and on the Nature of Historical Research." *International Migration Review* 1, no. 3 (Summer 1967): 5-9.

Georges, Robert A. and Stern, Stephen. *American and Canadian Immigrant and Ethnic Folklore. An Annotated Bibliography*. New York: Garland Publishing, 1982.

Gregorovich, Andrew. *Canadian Ethnic Groups Bibliography: A Selected Bibliography of Ethno-Cultural Groups in Canada and the Province of Ontario.* Toronto: Department of the Provincial Secretary and Citizenship of Ontario, 1972. xvi, 208pp. Section on "Italians," pp. 129-35.

Harney, Robert F. "Entwined Fortunes: Multiculturalism and Ethnic Studies in Canada." *Siirtolaisuss - Migration* 3 (1974-84): 68-94.

Harney, Robert F. "Frozen Wastes: The State of Italian Canadian Studies." In *Perspectives in Italian Immigration and Ethnicity*, pp. 115-31. Edited by S. Tomasi. New York: Center for Migration Studies, 1977.

Hurtubise, Pierre. "Il Canada negli archivi della congregazione de propaganda fide." *Il Veltro* 1-2, anno XXIX (January-April 1985): 107-13.

Hutcheon, Linda. "Italian Canadian Writings and the Canon: Integration or Ghetto-ization?" *Italian Canadiana* 2, no. 1 (Spring 1986): 31-37.

Italian Books/Libri Italiani: A Catalogue of the Holdings of the Languages Centre, Metropolitan Toronto Central Library. Toronto: Metro Toronto Library Board, 1973. 1 Vol.

Jansen, Clifford J. "The State of Italian-Canadian Research in North America." In *Italian Americans.* Edited by Lydio F. Tomasi. New York: Center for Migration Studies, 1985.

McLaren, Duncan. *Ontario Ethno-Cultural Newspapers, 1835-1972.* An Annotated Checklist. Toronto: University of Toronto Press, 1973. "Italians," pp. 97-111.

Mallea, John R., and Shea, Edward C. *Multiculturalism and Education: A Select Bibliography.* Informal Series 9. Toronto: Ontario Institute for Studies in Education and Ontario Ministry of Culture and Recreation, 1979. 292pp.

Malycky, Alexander. "University Research on Italian-Canadians: First Supplement." *Canadian Ethnic Studies* 5, nos. 1-2 (1973): 195-96.

Moquin, Wayne, with Van Doren, Charles, eds. *A Documentary History of the Italian Americans*. New York: Praeger. 448pp.

Palmer, Howard. "Canadian Immigration and Ethnic History in the 1970s and 1980s." *Journal of Canadian Studies* 17, no. 1 (Spring 1982): 35-50.

Palmer, Howard. "History and Present State of Ethnic Studies in Canada." In *Identities; The Impact of Ethnicity on Canadian Society*. Canadian Ethnic Studies Association Series Vol. 5, pp. 167-83. Edited by Wsevolod Isajiw. Toronto: Peter Martin, 1977.

Pane, Remigio U. "Doctoral Dissertations on the Italian American Experience." *International Migration Review* 9, no. 4 (Winter 1975): 545-56.

Pedreschi, Luigi. "Italian Publications in Canada 1965-1982: A Bibliography." *Canadian Geographer* 27 (1983): 279-84.

Perin, Roberto. "Clio as an Ethnic: The Third Force in Canadian Historiography." *Canadian Historical Review* 64, no. 4 (December 1983): 441-67.

Pivato, Joseph. "Canadian Women Writers of Italian Background." *Italian Canadiana* 2, no. 1 (Spring 1986): 38-49.

Pivato, Joseph, ed. *Contrasts: Comparative Essays on Italian-Canadian Writing*. Montreal: Guernica, 1985. 255pp Bibliography, pp. 231-46.

Pivato, Joseph. "Documenting Italian-Canadian Writing: A Bibliography." *Italian Canadiana* 1, no. 1 (Spring 1985): 28-37.

Pivato, Joseph. "Italian-Canadian Women Writers Recall History." *Canadian Ethnic Studies* 18, no. 1 (1986): 79-88.

Pivato, Joseph. "The Arrival of Italian-Canadian Writing." *Canadian Ethnic Studies* 14, no. 1 (1982): 127-37.

Ramirez, Bruno. "La recherche sur les Italiens du Quebec." *Questions de culture* 2 (1982): 103-11.

Rosoli, Gianfausto. "Sources and Current Research in Italy on Italian Americans." In *Perspectives in Italian Immigration and Ethnicity*, pp. 133-55. Edited by Silvano M. Tomasi. New York: Center for Migration Studies, 1977.

Rosoli, Gianfausto, and Ostuni, Maria Rosaria. "Laggio di bibliografia statistica dell'emigrazione italiana." In *Un secolo di emigrazione italiana: 1876-1976*, pp. 273-341. Edited by Gianfausto Rosoli. Rome: Centro Studi Emigrazione, 1978.

Scardellato, Gabriele P. *A Calendar of Documents of North American Interest in Various Series and Sub-Series of the 'Archivio Segreto Vaticano.'* Public Archives of Canada Microfiche Publication, Ms. Division Finding Aids, 1984.

Scardellato, Gabriele P. *A Calendar of Documents of North American Interest in the Series 'Francia,' Archives of the Secretary of State of the Holy See, 'Archivio Segreto Vaticano.'* Public Archives of Canada Microfiche Publication, Ms. Division Finding Aids, 1984.

Scardellato, Gabriele P., and Benoit, W.W. "The Flesh Made Word: The Vatican Archives and the Study of Canadian History, 1600-1799." *Archivaria* 20 (Summer 1985).

Seller, Maxine. "The Diversity of Italian America: New Materials from Arno Press – 'The Italian American Experience'." *Italian Americana* 2, no. 2 (Spring 1976): 255-69.

Tomasi, Silvano M., and Engel, Madeline H., eds. *The Italian Experience in the United States*. Staten Island, N.Y.: Center for Migration Studies, 1970. Selected Bibliography sections, pp. 39, 103, 210, 239.

Tomasi, Silvano M., and Stibili, Edward C. *Italian-Americans and Religion: An Annotated Bibliography*. New York: Center for Migration Studies, 1978. 222pp.

Vecoli, Rudolph J. "Emigration Historiography in Italy." *The Immigration History Newsletter* 6, no. 2 (1974): 1-5.

Vecoli, Rudolph J. "European Americans: From Immigrants to Ethnics." *International Migration Review* 6, no. 4 (Winter 1972): 403-34.

Vecoli, Rudolph J. "Return to the Melting Pot: Ethnicity in the United States in the Eighties." *Siirtolaisuus - Migration* 3 (1974-84): 117-27.

Winship, George Parker. *Cabot Bibliography*. London, 1900.

ADDENDUM

In the interval between compiling the present bibliography and its going to print, the following substantive works in Italian-Canadian Studies have been produced:

Perin, Roberto, and Sturino, Franc, eds. *Arrangiarsi: The Italian Immigrant Experience in Canada.* Montreal: Guernica, 1988.

Potestio, John, and Pucci, Antonio, eds. *The Italian Immigrant Experience.* Thunder Bay, Ontario: Canadian Italian Historical Association, 1988.

Zucchi, John E. *Italians in Toronto, 1875-1935.* Montreal: McGill-Queen's University Press, 1988.